The European Neutrals in International Affairs

Hanspeter Neuhold,
Hans Thalberg (eds.)

LONDON AND NEW YORK

First published 1984 by Westview Press, Inc.

Published 2019 by Routledge
52 Vanderbilt Avenue, New York, NY 10017
2 Park Square, Milton Park, Abingdon, Oxon OX14 4RN

Routledge is an imprint of the Taylor & Francis Group, an informa business

CIP-Kurztitelaufnahme der Deutschen Bibliothek

The European neutrals in international affairs/
Hanspeter Neuhold; Hans Thalberg
(eds.). — Wien: Braumüller, 1984.
(The Laxenburg Papers ; 7)
ISBN 3-7003-0609-1
NE: Neuhold, Hanspeter [Hrsg.]; GT

ISBN 13: 978-0-367-29187-7 (hbk)
ISBN 13: 978-0-367-30733-2 (pbk)

Contents

Contents

Editors' Preface

A conference, organized by the Austrian Institute for International Affairs and dealing with the topic "In Search of Peace and Security: The Role of the European Neutrals", was held at Schloß Laxenburg on 27 and 28 October 1983.

Three years earlier, on the occasion of the 25th anniversary of the establishment of Austria's permanent neutrality, the Institute had conducted a seminar on "Neutrality and Non-Alignment in Europe". The papers presented in 1980 were published as Laxenburg Paper no. 4 and served as the basis for the 1983 follow-up conference.

Whereas the main purpose then had been a comparison of various historic, political, legal, economic and military aspects of the neutral status of Austria, Finland, Sweden and Switzerland, and of the non-alignment of Yugoslavia, the conference in 1983 focused on two more specific topics.

On the one hand, scholars from the four neutral States of Europe dealt with what they regarded as their countries' main contributions to international peace and security, both on the European continent and at a global level. On the other hand, experts from selected non-neutral countries (Hungary, the Netherlands, Norway, the USA, the USSR and Yugoslavia) were invited to assess, in the eyes of their governments, of public opinion and in the literature on International Relations, the record of those four neutrals in the performance of the tasks for which they feel particularly qualified as a result of their neutral position. It was tempting indeed to ascertain whether the images which the governments and citizens of neutral States have of their countries' role in international relations are shared by others.

Not surprisingly, Austrian, Finnish, Swedish and the Swiss representatives emphasized different functions in the neutrality policies of their countries, given the historic, geostrategic, military and other differences among them. Yet, especially in the discussions following the presentations, common denominators were also stressed, above all the shift from (permanent) neutrality as a defensive strategy to keep States out of war to active efforts in peacetime to prevent and reduce international tension and a recent trend towards multilateral cooperation among non-bloc members, in particular within the framework of CSCE.

The divergent evaluations of neutrality by analysts from States belonging to military alliances or from a member of the non-aligned movement did not come as a surprise. The European neutrals must find the generally positive attitude towards their exceptional status among neighboring countries reassuring. They cannot but regret a certain "benign neglect", a lack of understanding of the functions which they can and which they can *not* fulfil, in other States, first and foremost among politicians and opinion leaders of the two Superpowers.

The authors were asked to update and revise their papers, if necessary, in the light of the debates at Schloß Laxenburg last year. In this volume the papers are presented in the order in which they were given last October. As Dr. Victor Kremenyuk had to cancel his participation literally almost at the last minute, Dr. Nicolai Polianow kindly agreed to state a Soviet point of view, which focused, however, only on Austria's permanent neutrality. Hence we decided to include Dr. Kremenyuk's more comprehensive paper, although it could not be discussed at the conference. Moreover, we felt that a summary of the main ideas expressed by the conference participants should be attempted. We therefore added a final chapter evaluating the results of the conference.

Thanks are due to the Nordic Cooperation Committee for International Politics, Stockholm, to the Klüber-Stiftung, Sarnen, and to the Embassy of the United States in Vienna for financial support to cover travel expenses of participants from their respective countries.

Finally, we want to thank the International Institute for Applied Systems Analysis for its generous hospitality during the conference and Mr. David Beal for his assistance in editing the papers. We hope that this second Laxenburg Paper on neutrality will—however modestly—increase interest in and understanding of a rather exceptional international status, from which not only the States endowed with it but others can benefit as well.

Pierre du Bois

Institut Universitaire d'Études Européennes, Geneva

Neutrality and Political Good Offices: The case of Switzerland

1. Introduction

There can be no Swiss foreign policy without good offices. Since the second half of the nineteenth century, Switzerland has considered its neutrality not only as the basis of its foreign policy but also as a "schedule of obligations" translated into a concept of active solidarity, particularly in the case of international conflict or controversy. For what is at stake is the credibility of neutrality abroad, especially with neighbor States. What would be the sense of neutrality without the advantages which it also bestows upon the international community?

Active neutrality implies diverse services which are the manifestation of the Swiss desire for solidarity. As Mr. Max Petitpierre, the former Swiss Minister for Foreign Affairs, declared in 1953, after the Federal Council had accepted to participate in the Neutral Nations Repatriation Commission in Korea and in the Neutral Nations Supervisory Commission, "Absolute and permanent neutrality, as we conceive and want it, is not defensible merely as abstention and passivity. It sometimes requires, if it is to be recognized and respected, the support of an action wich justifies it. Neutrality is an obligation[1]." In other terms, neutrality involves responsibilities. In January 1984, the Federal Council gave a reminder of this by emphasizing the commitment of the Confederation to peace in its *Bericht über die Richtlinien der Regierungspolitik 1983—1987*[2].

One of the responsibilities that neutrality implies is that of good offices. Whereas, in terms of public international law, good offices mean an action undertaken by a third State, an international organization or even a single citizen in order to procure a settlement between conflicting countries, in Switzerland this traditional legal concept is extended to include a wide range of activities which aims at bridging the gap in international controversies, at smoothing out difficulties resulting therefrom, at peacefully settling differences, or at least at alleviating conflicts, and in a more general way at helping to maintain peace among nations. It designates actions which are destined to somehow limit either other conflicts or differences between States or between States and national liberation movements.

Within the category of good offices, arbitration and mediation figure beside protection of foreign interests which consist in maintaining a minimum of contact between belligerents or between States which have broken off their diplomatic relations. The protection of prisoners of war and humanitarian actions—principally through the Red Cross —, hospitality to numerous international organizations or conferences, international mandates entrusted by the United Nations such as the participation of Switzerland in the Neutral Commissions in Korea or technical assistance in response to a request of the same United Nations, can also be considered within this category.

Unlike technical good offices, which do not suppose a real commitment, the political ones like mediation come up against two difficulties which necessarily limit their scope. On the one hand, a small State like Switzerland has not the means to pose as a mediator and a guarantor of peace on a world scale. On the other hand, the political risks involved in putting out peace feelers or offers of mediation dictate extreme caution. The necessity of keeping a strict attitude of non-intervention in every international crisis or conflict—a necessity enhanced by certain domestic political considerations—so as not to endanger neutrality itself, limits the Swiss authorities' possibilities for action in the international field.

Nevertheless, the evolution on the international scene, and in particular CSCE, opens to neutral countries—and in this case Switzerland—new possibilities for an active neutrality by allowing them to play a role as mediator or *"courtier"* between the two blocs. In the context of the international tensions that have been the rule over the past few years, the neutrals have been called to smooth tensions within the framework of CSCE, to facilitate negotiations in proposing compromises or "acceptable formulae", to use the term coined by Raymond Probst, former State Secretary for Foreign Affairs in Berne. Hence the often very strict limits of active neutrality do not exclude playing the beneficial role of "honest broker" on the international scene.

We can get a better idea of the reality of political good offices by the examination of concrete historical cases in which they have been performed.

2. The Meaning of Good Offices

The essential element of active neutrality lies in continually contributing to efforts to develop peaceful feelings between nations. The readiness of Switzerland to perform good offices is a constant of its foreign policy. From time to time the Federal Council reminds of its "wish to help in the solution of difficulties which might be the sources of tensions or conflicts whenever it can be of use within the limitations imposed by the respect for a strict neutrality". The policy of neutrality practiced by Switzerland has never led her to consider that she should, or could, not concern herself with international events in which she had not a direct interest; on the contrary, time has reinforced her conviction that "she should seize every available opportunity to associate herself with any effort across the globe which aims at the peaceful settlement of international disputes so as to help in the maintenance of peace". Such was the declaration on 28 November 1955 by Mr. Max Petitpierre before the Commission for Foreign Affairs of the Swiss States' Council[3].

This spirit of international solidarity also has its roots in the century-old tradition of humanitarian activity that has found its most visible reflection in the work of the International Committee of the Red Cross. Certain good offices rendered by the Swiss since the First World War have also been motivated by the desire to stop mass killings and catastrophic destruction or to help in a peace process. When Walter Stucki, the Swiss Minister in Vichy in 1944, offered to mediate between the Germans and collaborationists on one hand and the *Résistance* on the other, he did so to avoid the bombardment of the town of Vichy. The Swiss Consul-General in Bad Godesberg, von Weiss, played the same role between Germans and Americans in March 1945 in order to save the town from destruction. Two Swiss, Major Waibel and Zurich-born Max Husman, took the purely private initiative in Spring 1945 of trying to bring together the Americans and SS General Wolff, then *"Höchster SS- und Polizeiführer in Italien"*, to arrange an end to the war in Northern Italy, where the Germans were preparing massive destruction and where bloody confrontations had already taken place.
While remaining within the framework of neutrality as it were, the good offices or mediation suggested or carried out by the Swiss during the two World Wars in no way negated the immediate interests of the Confederation. Although Switzerland was spared the direct consequences of the conflicts, the Swiss nonetheless felt quite severely the economic effects of the hostilities—an experience to which other disagreeable burdens must be added. When Major Waibel spoke to Allen Dulles, the head of O.S.S. in Bern, at the beginning of 1945, Dulles recognized the "powerful and legitimate interest" of Switzerland in any plan that would lead to a rapid end of hostilities[4]. In this case the offers of good offices or mediation were amply justified by the risk of the destruction of the port of Genoa, where some Swiss goods had to transit, or by the risk to the industrial centers of Piedmont and Lombardy, where numerous Swiss firms had factories, or again by the risk of a huge and sudden influx of thousands of Nazi or fascist soldiers into the Confederation.

Moreover, certain Swiss statesmen were sometimes led by personal reasons of sentiment or ideology to undertake peace initiatives in the acknowledged or unconscious desire to bring together one group of belligerents at the expense of others. In the Spring of 1917, the head of the Political Department, Mr.

Hoffmann, tried to bring together Russia and Germany, for whom he had great sympathy. To bring this about he communicated to the Socialist Deputy, Robert Grimm, who was already in Petrograd, to sound out the Provisional Government on its peace plans and to impart to it confidental information on the aims of Germany and on its bargaining position in the case of negotiations taking place. Hoffmann even went so far as to affirm that "Germany will launch no offensive so long as a peaceful *entente* seems possible with Russia[5]." In 1943 the incumbent of the Political Department, Pilet-Golaz, greatly preoccupied by the danger of the Bolshevization of Europe, sounded out foreign diplomats in Bern, and in particular the Papal Nuncio, Bernardini, on a possible peace initiative which would "serve to avert the terrible consequences" of a Soviet victory[6].

What of considerations of prestige, even of vanity? Did they also play their part in the good offices or mediation attempted by the Federal Council, its representatives, or even in those of private citizens? Even if we cannot venture a definitive reply, the question is worth asking. In December 1916, the Federal Council let it be known that it was willing to offer its good offices in line with its "feeble possibilities". Professor Ruffieux claims that in this case Arthur Hoffmann, the instigator of the initiative, succumbed to personal vanity, much as did the newspapers that applauded the request of the Federal authorities[7]. The error of calculation demonstrated by the failure of this initiative was, in any event, proof of the irresponsibility or bluff that governed the offer of good offices. More recently there was the failure of the mediation efforts of the Confederation between the United States and Iran in the hostage crisis, a failure deeply felt by Berne, as is witnessed by the declarations of Swiss diplomats after the eventual release of the hostages, for which Algeria can take some of the credit. It is not to criticize Switzerland, or any other State, to point out the important role played by prestige in certain foreign policy initiatives.

One question that remains unanswered is that of legitimacy. How far is active neutrality a matter of domestic policy? While neutrality, in the strict sense of the word, is a necessity for reasons of the strategic situation and dependence on foreign countries, as well as a result of the needs of balance and of harmony between linguistic groups or parties, a more committed foreign policy runs the risk of creating more problems with public opinion, or even giving rise to actual protest. Thus, in some ways an active neutrality confers more legitimacy on foreign than on domestic policy, where account has to be taken of the ideology of consensus and restraint in matters of foreign policy.

But inversely, under certain circumstances, the Swiss Government is, so to speak, constrained by public opinion to abandon its discretion and to declare itself ready to serve the cause of peace. This happened in particular in 1969 during the Biafran Civil War. The emotional climate which reigned in Switzerland as a result of the massacres in Biafra induced the Swiss authorities to announce their readiness to offer their good offices and to undertake consultations with countries like—as the press reported—Austria, Sweden, Yugoslavia and Ethiopia with a view to a possible peace mission.

3. The Circumstances

First, good offices are requested or offered in time of general war, as was the case during the two World Wars. As we have mentioned, former Swiss Minister for Foreign Affairs, Arthur Hoffmann, tried in 1917 to bring about a separate peace between Germany and Russia after the collapse of Tsarism. Pilet-Golaz sounded out foreign diplomats in Berne in 1943 with a view to launching a peace initiative by the neutrals. Major Waibel, in 1945, succeeded in bringing together SS General Wolff and American delegates in order to accelerate the surrender of German armies in Northern Italy. On a more limited scale, the Swiss minister posted to Marshall Pétain's government, Walter Stucki, in 1944, and the Swiss consul in Cologne, von Weiss, in 1945, intervened to stop massive destructions in Vichy and in Bad Godesberg, respectively.

Secondly, good offices are asked for or proposed in case of conflict or tension between two States after diplomatic relations have broken down. Recently, from fall 1980 to spring 1981, Swiss diplomats acted as go-betweens in the Iranian hostage affair.

Lastly, mediation takes place in case of civil war or conflict between a State and a national liberation movement. The most famous example is that of the Swiss diplomat, Olivier Long, after December 1960, in bringing the Algerians of the FLN and the French to the negotiating table.

4. The Initiator

Who takes the initiative? There is no definite rule. The answer varies from case to case. Because of the risks involved in political good offices, the conflicting parties themselves usually ask for Swiss assistance. Such was the case in 1960, when an Algerian emissary, the delegate of the FLN in Rome, contacted Swiss representatives, asking them to act as go-betweens with the French. The process was the same in 1980 during the hostage affair. On this occasion, it was Washington which took the initiative in approaching Mr. Probst, then Ambassador to the United States.

In certain other circumstances, the initiative has been taken by the Swiss authorities or by a Swiss personality. In December 1916, the Federal Council decided to offer its good offices "in line with its feeble possibilities" to the belligerents. The initiative was more ambiguous in the case of Federal Councillor Hoffmann's telegram to the National Councillor Grimm in June 1917 in which the German war aims and the peace chances were made known. In 1943, Pilet-Golaz put out his own very shy peace feelers without informing his colleagues. Again, Stucki in Vichy and von Weiss in Bad Godesberg were the initiators of mediation between belligerents, as was Major Waibel between Wolff and the Americans.

5. "The Game Leader"

Who performs the mediatory function? This also depends on the circumstances. Sometimes, the Swiss authorities have been directly involved in the negotiation process—as in the hostage affair in Iran, where they intervented at the threefold level of the Embassy in Washington, the Department for Foreign Affairs in Berne and the Embassy in Tehran.

In other cases, a Swiss personality, with the agreement and assistance of the Swiss authorities or at least that of the Swiss Minister for Foreign Affairs, has been in charge of the negotiation. Long, supported by his Minister, Max Petitpierre, led the 1960/61 mediation between the FLN and France.

There remains the case where a Swiss national takes the first steps of mediation on his own initiative without referring to the Swiss government. This occurred in 1945 when Major Waibel decided on his own to accelerate the conclusion of peace in Northern Italy. The risks that the Swiss officer took with Swiss neutrality led to his ultimate censure.

6. The Principles

What are the principles governing political good offices? The first is to avoid endangering Swiss neutrality, in other words to avoid compromising the interests of one of the States involved in the conflict. Hoffmann's error in 1917 was not to have taken into account the interests of Russia's allies when he sent his telegram to Grimm, thus favoring Germany at the expense of the *Entente*. Hoffmann drew the consequences of his error and resigned. Although Pilet-Golaz' action did not immediately entail the same scandalous consequences, in the absence of a real official commitment, it nonetheless violated the rule of impartiality in suggesting to the Papal Nuncio in Bern an initiative by the neutrals in order to prevent, through a rapid peace, the Boshevization of Europe. When the Bolshevists learned of the Swiss Minister's actions, they were extremely annoyed. This incident was to prove one of the major reasons for the Soviet refusal to resume diplomatic relations with Switzerland in 1944—a refusal which led to Pilet-Golaz' resignation. The peace feelers of Major Waibel were similarly contrary to Soviet interests in so far as they could, in case of a separate peace in Northern Italy, accelerate the advance of American and British forces in the direction of Trieste.

Another principle is to safeguard the credibility of the Swiss government. Inopportune steps entail the risk of leading to a failure or to a snub. The 1916 declaration had no other result than that of a general negative reaction among all the belligerent parties. The invitation by the Federal Council in 1956 to France, Great Britain, the United States, the USSR and India after the Suez and Hungarian crises to an international conference was not much better received, both abroad and in Switzerland. "Against the interests—or in the absence of the interests—of the great powers, Switzerland cannot prevail. The Federal Council will not persist in its project[8]."

7. The Rules of the Game

The performance of good offices implies the observance of certain rules. The first of these is discretion. Without it, the whole process of mediation is menaced or at least compromised. Linked to this first rule, the second is the necessity of the absolute confidence of the parties to the conflict. This is achieved by manifesting total impartiality in the contacts, and convincing both parties of this. Another rule requires the capacity to explain the arguments of one conflicting party to the other and *vice versa.* This supposes a thorough knowledge of the facts of the case in question.

8. The Results

What are the results of political good offices? In Vichy and in Bad Godesberg, both Stucki and von Weiss succeeded in their efforts. They assured the safety of both towns which the hostilities menaced with destruction. To a certain extent, the Swiss Consul in Florence, Carlo Steinhäuslin, obtained the same result in 1944. Major Waibel contributed, not without difficulty or delay, to the surrender of the German forces in Northern Italy in 1945. Later on, in 1961/62, Long contributed successfully to the *rapprochement* between France and the FLN and to the conclusion of the Treaty of Evian which opened the door to the independence of Algeria.

In other cases, Swiss efforts resulted in failure or even complete fiasco. The best known example is that of Hoffmann in 1917. The hostages affair also has to be mentioned in this context. The failure in this case is due mostly to circumstances. The failure of the Americans in Iran and the victory of the Muslim fundamentalists in the April 1980 elections meant a change of climate in Tehran that rendered Ambassador Lang's mediation task impossible.

9. The Refusal of Good Offices

To refuse the role of mediator is often less costly than accepting it. Hoffmann's problems in 1917 illustrate the difficulties that can arise. During the Second World War, Switzerland avoided any action that might have entailed the risk of being compromised. In 1943, Pilet-Golaz as Foreign Minister refused to mediate between Badoglio's Italy and the Western Allies in order not to infringe upon the rights of Hitler's Germany. Another case shows this extreme Swiss caution: At the end of April 1945, the "Protector" of Bohemia and Moravia, Frank, told the Confederation, without consulting Hitler, that he was ready to throw all his forces into the fight against the Soviets and to offer no resistance to the Americans. What he asked was to be able to contact British and American representatives to discuss the protection of Czechoslovakia against Sovietization. As former Federal Councillor Petitpierre put it: "He wanted, in fact, the Federal Council to act as his intermediary with the British and Americans so that these latter might encourage German resistance at the expense of the Russians[9]." The Swiss authorities decided to do nothing. No one was informed of the initiative, and the note remained unanswered.

Inversely, good offices are sometimes refused by one or the other party—or even by both parties—to which they are offered. The recent case of the Biafran Civil War is worth mentioning. In 1969, after Colonel Ojukwu and a Swiss Member of Parliament, Ernesto Franzoni, had held secret talks, the Swiss Foreign Ministry confirmed in a statement that "Switzerland is always ready to extend her good offices if both sides request them, and if there seems a good chance of success". But both the Nigerian authorities and OAU rejected the offer[10].

10. Conclusions

What emerges in the light of history from a statistical point of view is the rarity of political good offices compared with the multiplicity of technical ones. Among these rare political cases—at the most twenty since 1848—, those that have been a success took place largely at a local level during the Second World

War, with the exception of various arbitrations between 1870 and 1914 and Long's actions in 1960/62. The failures—especially attempts at peace-making or international *détente*—are illustrative of the enormous difficulties faced by a small State engaged in the peace-making process on a broad scale, given the relative weakness of the means at its disposal, but also due to the complexity inherent in the process of mediation in the absence of a consensus among the adversaries. Considerations of domestic politics can also affect the Swiss ability to intervene in certain cases.

While in the case of technical good offices no such obstacles exist, since they do not require a political commitment, in the case of "mediation" the situation is completely different. The principles Switzerland has to observe owing to its neutral status and the resulting risks of every engagement call for extreme caution in international activities. Neutral States are sometimes tempted to intervene as mediator or peace-maker in times of conflict or tension—be it under the pressure of public opinion, motivated by moral principles or in their search for international consideration or prestige. They may tend to overlook the limited power potential at their disposal and the risks they run of endangering their very neutrality.

An adequate policy seems to rely, first, on the correct evaluation of a neutral State's own interests and means. The leaders of neutral States have to assess their capacity to influence others correctly. It does not mean they cannot intervene, but they can intervene only under certain circumstances and if certain conditions are met.

What is more, because of the increasing interdependence of all nations, there is another field—an open field—where diplomats of neutral countries have the opportunity of contributing to the search for solutions or compromises. This is in the framework of such international negotiations as CSCE, as has been demonstrated in the 70s. The agreement obtained in Madrid in 1983 owes much to their mediatory activities. Their relatively new role in international fora is not their smallest contribution to the functioning of today's international system.

Notes

1 Max Petitpierre (ed.), Seize ans de neutralité active. Aspects de la politique étrangère de la Suisse (1945—1961) (Neuchâtel 1980), p. 298.
2 See Neue Zürcher Zeitung, January 27, 1984.
3 See Raymond Probst, Die "guten Dienste" der Schweiz (Berne 1958), p. 172.
4 See Allen Dulles, Les secrets d'une reddition (Paris 1967), p. 98.
5 Jacques Freymond/Isabelle Graf-Junod/Alison Browning (eds.), Documents diplomatiques suisses (vol. 6, Berne 1981), p. 563.
6 Pierre Blet/Robert A. Graham/Angelo Martini/ Burkhart Schneider (eds.), Actes et documents du Saint Siège relatifs à la Seconde Guerre mondiale (vol. 7, Vatican City 1973), p. 225.
7 Roland Ruffieux, La Suisse de l'entre-deux-guerres (Lausanne 1974), p. 46.
8 Jacques Freymond, La Suisse face aux conflits, in: Max Petitpierre (ed.), op. cit., p. 149.
9 Max Petitpierre parle, in: Tribune de Genève, 6 juin 1980.
10 See Colin Legum, International Involvement in Nigeria 1966—1970, in: Yashpal Tandon/Dilshad Chandarana (eds.), Horizons of African Diplomacy (Nairobi 1974), p. 79.

Karl Zemanek

Institute of International Law and International Relations, University of Vienna

Austria's Policy of Neutrality: Constants and Variables

1. Introduction

a) Role and Function

When I first read the title of this conference, to which I should contribute a paper from the Austrian point of view, I was uncertain about its meaning. What disturbed me most, was the word "role" which, according to the Oxford Dictionary, means "the part or character which one untertakes, assumes". This definition strongly suggests a self-chosen activity. But were there any roles from which a neutral State could choose while searching for peace and security? And if that were the case, was there any freedom of choice?

In my opinion, Austrian neutrality can only be understood as a function—in the mathematical sense—of a power conflict. In mathematics a function regards a variable quantity in its relation to one or more other variables on the value of which its own value depends. The "one or more variables" are the conflicting powers. In relation to their conflict, neutrality has a "function" within the ordinary meaning of the term, which is given by the Dictionary as "a specific purpose of an entity or its characteristic action". Thus, function merits our attention more than role, because it is in the context of the former that the latter can be developed.

I was therefore relieved when reading in an accompanying circular letter the instruction to present "the main aspects" of Austria's neutral policy, which broadens the scope considerably. At the same time, it creates a different problem: To present the main aspects of Austria's neutral policy in detail would require a book. Since that is not expected in the present context, I had two options: either to concentrate on a few (hopefully) important aspects or to present an overall but very superficial picture. I opted for the first approach.

b) Constants and Variables

For this analysis the tools of "role" and "function" seem not particularly well suited. They have a dogmatic, prescriptive flavor, whereas foreign policy, even that of a neutral State, is primarily determined by interests, not by prescriptions. Thus, while it may be possible, from a theoretical point of view, to prescribe a certain policy as best suiting a particular "role" or "function", the policy-makers of the neutral or of other concerned powers may not see it that way.

Moreover, I assume that my paper should not focus on how Austria's policy should look but, rather, how it actually does look. I propose, therefore, a more empirical approach, for which other analytical tools are needed. Such tools are "constants" and "variables", for which I shall probe Austria's policy of neutrality.

It may seem, on first hearing these terms, that "constants" are identical with "functions" and "variables" with "roles". Although there is some coincidence, because both sets of terms are applied to the same phenomena, the focus is different.

As a working hypothesis, I use the term "constants" for what appear, over a longer period of observation, *unchanging objectives* of Austria's policy of neutrality, whereas "variables" are factors which influence *in varying degrees at different times* the policies that are designed to achieve these objectives.

2. Constants

a) Stabilizing Relations in Central Europe

This is probably the best, if not the only, example of an Austrian neutral "function". For understanding it properly, it will help to have a short look at the historical situation existing before and in 1955.

After the Second World War two opposing power groups emerged in Europe. The dividing line between their respective zones of influence, if continued on Austrian territory, would have cut the country in two. What militated against the impending danger of partition was the strong determination of the Austrian people who could, fortunately, express themselves, from as early as 1945 onward, through a freely elected Government. The opposing groups, on the other hand, were determined not to leave the whole of Austria to the other side. The Soviet Union feared that an independent Austria might join NATO and, because of her geographic location, become a threat to her security. The USA and other Western powers feared that an independent Austria, because of her geographic location, might soon be swallowed up in the Soviet bloc. The strategic stalemate favored Austria's establishing herself as a permanently neutral country by offering reasonable guarantees that she would not involve herself in the East-West-conflict once the occupation ended. Although this fell short of the goals which each power group presumably wished to achieve, it at least prevented the achievement of the rival goal. These were the circumstances under which Austria's permanent neutrality became acceptable to both groups[1].

By taking herself out of the East-West game as an active player, Austria made the establishment of the Central European and East Central European neutral belt between NATO and the Eastern bloc countries possible. Her main contribution to peace in Europe, and thereby to international peace, lies in this disengagement of forces in the area. Her stabilizing function consists, therefore, in maintaining her neutral existence, thereby preventing conflict spillover from one area to the other.

From a political point of view, a successful discharging of this stabilizing function requires an adequate management of crisis situations occurring in the neighborhood, since both sides are watching the reactions of the permanently neutral country carefully. It appears that Austria has stood the test in 1956 (Hungary)[2], in 1968 (Czechoslovakia)[3], and—although affected only distantly—in 1981/82 (Poland).

From a strategic point of view, two variables have to be considered. One is the balance of forces between the opposing power groups in Europe. Austria has the greatest interest in the stability of this balance, because it minimizes the danger of the outbreak of an armed conflict. Such a conflict, when fought with nuclear weapons, would not stop at the neutral's border since atoms, once set free, know of no neutrality. We note, therefore, with grave concern that those States which station on their territories missiles with nuclear warheads, targeted at the central European area, are apparently prepared to violate Austria's neutrality as a result of their eventual use.

A stable balance of forces is, therefore, a necessity for the peaceful existence of the neutrals. Yet they have very limited possibilities of assisting in its maintenance or of preventing an arms race between the Superpowers as a potentially destabilizing event. Bilaterally, such possibilities do not exist at all. Whether the neutrals can exercise influence multilaterally is the subject of examination in the next chapter.

The other variable is the military potential of the neutral. Stabilizing an area without adequate means of defense is impossible. It is the defensive strength of the neutral which gives credibility to its assertion of maintaining neutrality under all circumstances. Since this implies a defensive strategy, its foremost requirement is that the people identify with their society and its institutions and with the neutral existence of their nation to the point that they will resist any foreign attempt at changing it by force, by all means available to them.

This observation does not diminish the importance of adequate defensive weapons; nor can it be denied that Austria has certain problems in this respect. But the history of the last decades proves that it is the unswerving resolution to resist which determines, in the last instance, the price of aggression.

b) Participation in the Multilateral Process

Austria's intensive and special involvement in the multilateral processes in the contemporary international system is the nearest example of a self-chosen neutral "role" that one can find. It is also the activity in which the Swiss and Austrian policies of neutrality differ most remarkably.

If one searches for the cause of this difference, it might again be useful to make a short historical excursion. When Austria regained her independence and adopted neutrality in 1955, she faced a twofold task: re-establishing herself on the international scene from which she had been absent for 17 years; and seeking recognition for her newly-acquired status. Not recognition in a formal legal sense, which had been forthcoming from all members of the international community; but recognition in a political sense, as a useful and indispensable member of the international community in her new existence. It was felt that membership in the United Nations[4] would at one and the same time add to Austria's security and provide an opportunity to build her profile as a neutral State for the greatest number of States in the shortest possible time. The situation was, therefore, significantly different from that of Switzerland, with its long tradition of neutrality and its tight net of bilateral representation.

But the task was not easy because Austria was herself yet in a learning stage on matters of neutrality. In an early period refuge was excessively sought in abstentions. It took some time to understand that a non-partisan position on matters of principle, like the use of force or human rights, was politically possible if maintained consistently against violations from all quarters[5]. It was not abstention on such matters that the other States expected from permanently neutral Austria.

What they did expect was the active use of her independence from existing blocs and groupings in establishing lines of communication between opposing interests and assistance in the search for solutions. It would be preposterous to suggest that this had anything to do with mediation in the traditional sense. For mediation, neutral States, and Austria in particular, lack the political weight necessary to edge the parties into a proposed solution. The neutrals can only act when the parties are basically interested in a solution. Then, however, they may play a useful role as brokers of ideas which either side, considering its image abroad or at home, might find difficult to accept when labelled as coming from the other side.

I think that this point is best illustrated by the activity of the so-called n+n group at the different sessions of CSCE: In Geneva and in Madrid, where such a basic interest in a result existed, they could play a useful role. In Belgrade the situation was different.

The example of CSCE shows that the interest in specific neutral services on the multilateral level is no longer limited to the United Nations. This is a consequence of the growing multilaterization of the world process which extends to all areas, with the exception of the direct security relations between the two Superpowers. I submit that neutral activities in this multilateral process have largely replaced the once heralded good offices of and mediation by neutral States in bilateral relations. This does not imply that neutrals may not sometimes play a role in bilateral tensions, for instance as protecting powers, when diplomatic relations are suspended or broken off. But it seems hardly credible that the international community would maintain their singular status and respect their privileges for that reason alone.

I suggest that today an appropriate activity of neutral States in the multilateral process is expected. Whether that activity can be useful depends on the intentions of the parties involved. But I submit that this activity is indispensable and can neither be carried out by States that are members of a pact system nor by the group of non-aligned countries, since that group is too heterogeneous and has too many interests of its own.

2. Variables

a) Political Parties

The most obvious factor to be considered in this context are Austria's political parties. Austria is a democratic State. And although it is a pluralistic society, there exists a broad political consensus on basic values such as human rights, the rule of law and social market-economy. Ideologically, Austria is thus part of the Western World.

Since the re-establishment of an independent Austria, a "common foreign policy" has been axiomatic between her major political forces. As long as the country was governed by a coalition of its two major political parties, the Christian-Democrats and the Social Democrats, reality coincided more or less with this axiom, since the two parties had to settle their differences within the government.

And differences there were and are[6]. Usually, however, these do not originate in disagreement over basic values or aims as found in party programs. They are more truly the product of day-to-day politics and therefore incidental rather than immanent. One can, nevertheless, locate a few relatively stable sources of friction in some characteristic features of modern political parties, as the two following examples show.

One is the growing internationalization of party politics. The two major Austrian parties participate in movements of like-minded political parties, i. e. the Socialist International and the International Democratic Union, respectively. Within those movements views on major world issues, such as disarmament or the North-South dialogue, or on crisis areas, like the Middle East and Central America, are formed under the influence of majorities from non-neutral countries. Sometimes common initiatives are undertaken. These views and initiatives may or may not coincide with a neutral's best interests; but even if they don't, group solidarity will be a strong incentive for a party from a neutral country not to break ranks.

Nor is this the only influence of international affiliation. When a party evaluates another country's international actions it will, together with other considerations, take into account who is governing in that country. When it happens to be a sister party, sympathy may, not unnaturally, tint the view.

Another characteristic feature of modern political parties is their different sensibility to outside influence. With an eye on their potential electorate and because of their traditional structures and their roles as government or opposition, Austrian parties react differently to efforts by organized interest groups or grassroot movements to influence their policies. Since some important international issues, like peace, disarmament, or the protection of the environment, are currently the subject of such pressures, different reactions contribute to different stands of the respective parties.

Such differences have come into the open since 1966 when the old coalition was replaced by a one-party government and foreign policy became a subject of debate between Opposition and Government in Parliament and in other bodies concerned with foreign or security policy. Their public airing is favored by the growing tendency to consider foreign policy mainly in the light of domestic policy—a phenomenon which plagues all democratic regimes. Thus, the government sees foreign policy also—and sometimes exclusively—as a means to embellish its image among the electorate, which is rarely informed enough to judge events independently. And the Opposition regards Government foreign policy with the same objectives in mind, although, of course, with its own image in view.

This leads to the conclusion that there is a basic consensus among all political parties on the long-range objectives of Austria's policy of neutrality, which have been described as "constants" in the first part of this paper. To this extent one can speak of a "common foreign policy". One should, however, be aware that different Austrian governments have—and may in the future—put stress on policies which serve those objectives differently.

b) Personalities

A consideration of the variables in Austria's policy of neutrality would be incomplete if it did not include a reference to some political personalities who, during their periods of office, have profoundly influenced this policy. I need only mention Chancellor Julius Raab who was the driving force behind the events that led to Austria's neutrality in 1955.

During the last 13 years, the foreign policy of Austria and with it the policy of neutrality were dominated by Chancellor Bruno Kreisky. Through his manyfold initiatives, his enormous international prestige, accumulated during a long activity, and through his—during a certain period (together with Palme and Brandt)—dominating position in the Socialist International, he gave Austria a political profile far beyond her potential.

Some of his more spectacular initiatives have been wrongly associated with Austria's policy of neutrality; they were simply the fruit of a very personal diplomacy. It should be apparent that such things as involvement in the Middle East and North Africa, in Central America and in other crisis areas of the world are not repeatable under changed circumstances.

This does not imply that Austria will not continue her active policy of neutrality. But it may be expected that this policy will be more confined to the "constants" described in the first part of this paper.

Notes

1 For the history of the period see Gerald Stourzh, The Austrian State Treaty and the Origins of Austrian Neutrality, Austria Today 3/83, pp. 17, and other works of the same author cited here. Relevant documents have been published by Alfons Schilcher, Österreich und die Großmächte; Dokumente zur österreichischen Außenpolitik 1945—1955 (Vienna and Salzburg 1980); and Ministerium für Auswärtige Angelegenheiten der UdSSR, UdSSR—Österreich 1938—1979, Dokumente und Materialien (Moscow 1980).

2 For the events and their handling see Felix Ermacora, 20 Jahre österreichische Neutralität (Frankfurt/Main 1975), pp. 94ff; Manfried Rauchensteiner, Spätherbst 1956. Die Neutralität auf dem Prüfstand (Vienna 1981).

3 See Hanspeter Neuhold, Karl Zemanek, Die Österreichische Neutralität im Jahre 1968, 9 Österreichische Zeitschrift für Außenpolitik (1969), pp. 156; Ermacora, op. cit., pp. 144.

4 See Karl Zemanek, Neutral Austria in the United Nations, 15 International Organization (1961), pp. 408; Wolfgang Strasser, Österreich und die Vereinten Nationen (Vienna and Stuttgart 1967).

5 See Karl Zemanek, Dauernd neutrale Staaten in den Vereinten Nationen, 18 Österreichische Zeitschrift für Außenpolitik (1978), pp. 264.

6 See Konrad Ginther, Neutralität und Neutralitätspolitik (Vienna and New York 1975).

Harto Hakovirta

Institute of Political Science, University of Tampere

An Interpretation of Finland's Contributions to European Peace and Security*

1. Introduction

In the study of neutral States' contributions to international peace and security, there is always the risk of committing either of the two following fallacies: On the one hand, cynical realism may lead one to look upon all small States as powerless pawns on the chessboard of Great Power politics. From such a point of view, a small neutral State's possibilities to contribute to regional or global peace and security appear, of course, negligible. On the other hand, seen from within a small neutral State, its potential for inducing or preventing changes in the international system or some sub-system is easily exaggerated because attention is naturally focussed in a more or less biased way on those particular system variables where some influence by the State concerned would be most likely to be discerned. Perhaps the only way to cope with the latter problem is just to keep oneself fully aware of its possibility. The fallacy of power realism can perhaps be avoided, at least to some extent, by allowing some variation in the kinds and degrees of contributions.

Thus, it may prove useful to distinguish between direct vs. indirect, unilateral vs. collateral or cooperative, and specific vs. general or diffuse contributions. Or, in other words, it may sometimes be meaningful to speak of the contribution of a small neutral State to international peace and security even if that State were able to influence the international system or a regional sub-system only indirectly, together or in cooperation with other States and through continuous policies rather than some spectacular political initiative or intervention. Moreover, it might, in some analytical contexts, be appropriate to assess the latent potential of a State to play roles in international security and peace-making efforts even if its historical record in such activities were only modest. Finally, all States influence the structures and processes of peace and security in the international system even

* While I remain responsible for possible errors of fact and interpretation, I am indebted to Ambassador Jaakko Iloniemi for valuable comments on the first draft of this paper.

regardless of their motives. Sometimes "peace policies" may produce international conflicts, and policies based solely or primarily on "selfish national interest" may produce peaceful effects. If only intentional and specific peace policies are taken into account, the analysis of the impact of a State on international peace and security may miss essential points.

The purpose of the present essay is the analysis and assessment of Finland's contributions to European peace and security during the post-Second World War era. The discussion will be structured around the following five themes: the stability of Finland's international position, Finland's role in the context of Nordic security, Finland's "bridge-builder" role, Finland's role in CSCE, and Finland's role in European image politics.

The term "role" means here roughly the same as "functions", "contributions" and "performances". In other words, it does not primarily refer to the expectations other States have of Finland in the field of regional peace and security, although even this "social-psychological" aspect will be touched upon.

The term "European peace and security" is assumed to be roughly defined by its constituent words. It is used as a general topic of discussion rather than as an analytical concept. To the extent necessary, its specific meanings will be illuminated from the Finnish point of view.

2. The Stability of Finland's International Position

Perhaps the most important contribution a country like Finland can make to European peace and security is to maintain a state of peace and stability in its own international position. In this respect, Finland's starting point at the end of the Second World War was not promising. In fact, Finland, together with Yugoslavia and perhaps Ireland, was the only significant unstable element in the new Europe characterized from the late 1940s onwards by two fairly rigid alliance systems, a couple of firmly neutral countries and occupied Germany and Austria. The eventual solutions to the German and Austrian issues were bound to be inextricably linked with the East-West division. Moreover, no capitalist State had yet experiences of an actively cooperative relationship with the Soviet Union, and Finland's earlier experiences with her big Eastern neighbor were of a negative nature. On the other hand, it was widely assumed in the West during the early Cold War years that the Soviet Union would soon occupy Finland or otherwise establish her domination over this country. The conclusion of the Treaty of Friendship, Cooperation and Mutual Assistance between Finland and the USSR in 1948 in particular evoked such speculations in the USA and other Western countries. It would, of course, be an exaggeration to say that these kinds of instabilities in Finland's international position created a risk of general European war at the time, since it was widely recognized that the West, though sympathetic to Finland, would not have risked a war or even a severe crisis with the Soviet Union for the sake of this country. Anyhow, Finland was one of the few places in Europe where the stability of the whole region was regarded as being in jeopardy. The instabilities in the Yugoslavian position were, of course, even more dangerous in this respect.

The main aspects of the stabilization of Finland's international position since then can be summed up in three points.[1]

First, Finland has been able to establish a durable *modus vivendi* in terms of security and opposed social systems, as well as a cooperative functional relationship with the Soviet Union. No severe political crises have occurred in Finnish-Soviet relations since the "night frosts" in 1958/59 and the "note crisis" in 1961, even in times of increasing East-West tensions. It could perhaps be said that the parties have already tested the limits of their relations sufficiently in this respect. Their experiences of mutual functional cooperation and exchange have no doubt been predominantly positive. Given the basic differences in the social systems of the two countries and the latent incompatibilities between the military provisions of the 1948 Treaty and Finland's efforts towards neutrality, tensions can probably never be totally eliminated from Finnish-Soviet relations. However, so long as the two countries are able to settle their occasional disputes through bilateral negotiations—as they have been thus far—these tensions are not likely to spill over to the wider areas of European and East-West politics.

Second, despite her unpromising starting point Finland has been able to establish a fairly recognized position of neutrality in the East-West conflict. Up to the mid-1950s, this effort was latent in Finland's foreign policy, but since then the country has persistently tried to make it well-known and internationally accepted. By the early 1960s, she had acquired recognition for her policy of neutrality. And since the late 1960s, this policy has gained increasing international respect within the context of Finland's performances in the field of peace policies. The fact that Finland is committed to conditional and limited military cooperation with the Soviet Union in particular conditions of war qualifies her neutrality considerably. This has not, however, essentially reduced her possibilities of pursuing a recognized policy of neutrality since the awareness of these commitments is an inherent element in the recognitions given to that policy by Eastern and Western powers. Even apart from such basic recognition, Finland has been increasingly accepted as a full-fledged member of the circle of European neutral States. Among the most illuminating indications of this position are her negotiations with the European Community at the beginning of the 1970s concurrently with Switzerland, Austria and Sweden, and her close cooperation with these neutral States within the context of the CSCE.

Third, through coordinating her relations with the USSR and her policy of neutrality, Finland has been able to simultaneously solve her main security problem and establish such possibilities for international cooperation and exchanges as the objective premises of her vital economic interests and the mixed political and cultural identities of the Finns permit. This is important even for Europe as a whole, because one of the basic preconditions for durable international stability on this continent is that the foreign policies of the European States be based on broad and permanent popular support and that stability and order in these countries be maintained. The requirements of political stability within and between States may, of course, come into conflict with those of social progress and lasting peace in international relations, but this general point is hardly relevant in the case of Finland and her foreign relations.

It is, moreover, worthwhile emphasizing in this connection that Finland's peace efforts have also been based on her ability to coordinate her relations with the East with her neutral posture into an internationally and domestically acceptable whole, rather than on either of these components alone.

Given the topic of this conference and this paper, I have mainly highlighted the positive aspects of Finland's international position and foreign policy. The same historical developments could, of course, be analyzed from a more critical point of view. For the same reason, I may also have overemphasized Finland's own merits in the stabilization of her international position. Nevertheless, it seems to me that Finland has done her greatest service to European peace and security by successfully managing her own affairs in a relatively difficult geostrategic position; at least so satisfactorily that she has not become an area of confrontation between East and West. Today Finland is one of the most stable countries in Europe. Both East and West seem to favor the continuation of her present policies. In this sense, Finland has become an institutionalized component of the European system of States.

3. Finland and Nordic Security

Finland's contribution to European peace and security follows partly from her position and performances in the Nordic context. Above all, she plays her role in the Nordic "Security Community". This Deutschian term refers primarily to the fact that the Nordic countries have been able to eliminate the threat of military aggression from their mutual relations so definitively that their international sub-system appears as a civilized island of peace in the otherwise predominantly anarchic international system of States[2]. This picture is, of course, to some extent idealized in the sense that it does not sufficiently take into account either the possibilities of Nordic conflicts due to the Norwegian, Danish, and Icelandic commitments to NATO as opposed to Finland's military commitments to the Soviet Union, or of the spill-over of East-West tensions into this region. The fact remains nevertheless that the Nordic region is, politically, perhaps the most stable, and militarily, the most secure part of Europe, where at least the genuinely internal potential for military confrontations has been minimized. In addition, the Nordic countries have shown considerable restraint and mutual solidarity in areas or matters in which their international orientations are incompatible.[3]

Finland has taken more initiatives to promote Nordic peace and security than the Scandinavian countries[4]. The roots of Finland's endeavors in this field can be traced back to 1952 when Prime Minister Kekkonen first discussed the possibility of extended cooperation between "neutral Nordic countries"[5]. Since then, Finland's foreign policy authorities have occasionally spoken of the benefits of Nordic neutrality or disengagement, although they generally share the common Nordic view that the basic foreign policy choices of each country in the region must be respected by the others. The second major step in Finland's Nordic peace policy was taken in 1961 when, in connection with the Soviet-Finnish "note crisis", she adopted the task of monitoring the development of the security situation in Northern Europe and the Baltic area and informing the Soviet government of her views on required actions[6]. This vaguely defined role, however, evoked interest in Scandinavia for only a few years, and its relevance for Finnish-Soviet relations may also have diminished since then. The most significant and best known of Finland's Nordic initiatives concerns, of course, the establishment of a Nordic nuclear-free zone, which has been one of the major themes in Finland's peace policy since it was first introduced in 1963[7]. Moreover, in 1963, President Kekkonen proposed the demilitarization of the Finnish-Norwegian border area by means of a bilateral treaty. President Koivisto has admitted that it may be difficult to agree on such a formal treaty. But the idea itself could, according to him, be partly realized by unambiguous and parallel political declarations by Finland and Norway.[8]

But has Finland's factual contribution to Nordic peace and security through these various proposals and roles been greater than that of the Scandinavian countries? If only the concrete results as opposed to declared intentions are taken into account, the answer seems to be "no". In fact, Finland may even have caused some minor tensions in this region by making proposals and adopting roles which she knows are not acceptable to her neighbors.[9] Of course, Finland has not adopted such policies in order to strain her relations with her Scandinavian neighbors; her views of how Nordic security could best be promoted are conditioned by her position as neighbor and treaty partner of the USSR, just as those of Norway and Denmark are conditioned by their membership of NATO and those of Sweden by her less exposed and less dependent position.

However, although Finland's initiatives within the Nordic context have not produced any treaties, they need not to have been useless. Above all, these initiatives have contributed to the political foundations of the non-nuclear status quo in the Nordic region by keeping the Scandinavian countries aware of Finland's automatic opposition to any policies aiming at a change in this respect and by providing a point of reference for Nordic security debates. It is, moreover, important to note that since Finland's Nordic initiatives and roles have also largely coincided with the peace policy interests of the Soviet Union, they have helped Finland's endeavors to develop good relations with this Great Power. This, in turn, was assumed above to be essential for the stability of Finland's position in the European system of States. Finally, Finland's Nordic initiatives have demonstrated to the Finns that their government is doing its best to promote the nation's security and have thus contributed to the domestic support for the country's foreign policy. If a Nordic nuclear-weapon-free zone were to be established in the future, it would certainly have a significant impact on European peace and security. A detailed discussion of this matter would, however, be beyond the scope of this paper.

4. Finland's Role as a "Bridge-Builder"

An important enlargement of Finland's international peace role occurred in 1961 when President Kekkonen, in his New Year's speech, launched the idea of Finland's role as a "bridge-builder" between East and West, thus making use of her unique international location. Towards the end of the decade, Finland's self-confidence in this respect had increased considerably. In a speech in 1967, President Kekkonen went so far as to relate Finland's model as "bridge-builder" to desires, recently expressed by the NATO Council of Ministers, for an intensification of Western contacts with Eastern Europe[10]. Somehow this self-imposed "bridge-builder" role dominated, along with the narrower Nordic roles, Finland's peace policies until the late 1960s, when it began to be overshadowed by her activities in connection with SALT and above all CSCE. Finland has never explicitly abandoned her "bridge-builder" ambition. However, she has not insisted on this theme in her declaratory policies since the 1960s. Nowadays, it has come up mostly indirectly in some of Finland's responses to the debate of "Finlandization" to which I shall return in Section 6.

It is possible to imagine various kinds of "bridge-building" performances by neutral States in East-West relations, ranging from involvement as a third party in a bloc dispute to active functional relations with East European countries. Finland's characterizations of her "bridge-builder" role have clearly tended towards the latter end of this scale. The Finnish decision-makers have explicitly stressed that Finland had no ambitions to intrude as a non-invited mediator or arbiter in Great Power conflicts. Even the idea that Finland could build some bridges of functional cooperation from, say, the USSR to the USA is obviously too demanding. The only realistic possibility is that Finland, as a country with

Western institutions, could contribute a plank of an East-West bridge by her own relations to the East and the value of those relations as a model. How has she performed in this respect?

No doubt, Finland has been an outstanding pioneer in developing functional relations with the Soviet Union as far as the conclusion of long-term trade and cooperation agreements is concerned. Her share in total Western trade with the USSR has also been much higher than might be expected on the basis of her economic potential. Further, Finland has shown particular sensitivity to the problems of East-West economic relations when concluding agreements with West European economic organizations. At the same time, she has shown responsiveness to the expectations of the Soviet Union concerning compensatory arrangements in such cases. Most important of all, perhaps, is the fact that Finland provided a potential precedent in Western economic relations with Eastern Europe when she concluded a treaty on economic cooperation with CMEA in 1973[11].

On the other hand, Finland's performances are more of a negative than positive model value in some other respects. Thus, for example, she has on the whole liberalized her Eastern trade to a lesser extent than many other Western countries; her trade and other economic relations with East-European countries other than the USSR have remained on a comparatively low level; and her Eastern trade as a whole is qualitatively less balanced than that of, say, Switzerland, Austria, or Sweden. It could also perhaps be said that the Finnish government has not been particularly active in developing industrial cooperation with Eastern Europe, as, for example, an analysis of relevant patent exchange statistics would seem to suggest[12]. Compared with other neutral countries, Finland's performances as a "bridge-builder" in East-West functional cooperation are, on the whole, perhaps most outstanding, but it would be misleading to claim that they are outstanding in every respect. In some significant respects they are in fact more negative than positive. Besides, Finland's particular performances in developing economic relations with the Soviet Union are mostly due to her international position which no other State could imitate. In propagating the model value of her position and performances in relation to the Soviet Union, Finland perhaps more easily evokes irritation than attracts interested followers.

All in all, Finland's factual preconditions for playing the role of a "bridge-builder" in East-West relations may be more modest than the country's foreign policy-makers initially assumed. This could be part of the explanation for the gradual disappearance of this theme from Finland's peace policy rhetoric.

5. Finland's Role in the CSCE

Finland's international role was expanded considerably at the end of the 1960s when she opened discussions with the European and North American countries on the CSCE in May 1969 and when the USA and the USSR opened the negotiations on SALT I in Helsinki in November, 1969. The following analysis focusses on Finland's role in CSCE, since SALT was more a matter of Superpower than European politics, and since Finland's role as one of the two hosts of the SAL negotiations was technical rather than political. It is, however, obvious that the positive international attention gained by Finland in connection with SALT was an asset in her efforts to complete the preparations for the CSCE.

High international tensions are not only a general security risk for Finland. High tensions also entail the danger of Finland's international position becoming an object of intensive international speculations and, as a consequence, her external freedom of action becoming more circumscribed. At the same time, this may lead to more domestic demands that the government should do something in the name of national and international security. Finland's position is obviously more vulnerable than that of the other neutral European States, whose positions are more secure and whose freedom of action is mainly based on other kinds of determinants. Moreover, high international tensions tend to focus international attention in Europe on the political, economic and cultural divisions of this continent and consequently also highlight the limitations and weaknesses in Finland's international position. On the other hand, increasing exchanges and cooperation across bloc boundaries within the context of *détente* tend to highlight Finland's potential for positive international contributions and to enhance her security.[13]

There is a basic difference in the nature of the foreign policy resources of Finland, on the one hand, and those of, above all, Switzerland and Sweden on the other. The latter countries' resources are mainly internal, consisting, first of all, of a relatively favorable international location, a long tradition of neutrality, and fairly strong national military deterrence. Of course, the reduction of international tensions, at least to a modest level, is beneficial to them also since it decreases the danger of war and increases the scope of international activities in which a neutral State can participate. However, some degree of passivity and isolation in times of high tension is by no means fatal to their international interests or their chances of adopting a new, more active policy when tension is again reduced. Both countries have been able to play international third-party roles although they have often been critical of the policies of the Great Powers. Finland, for her part, is more dependent on the external acceptability of her foreign policy and her ability to gain prestige through repeated positive performances in peace politics. Her chances of obtaining suitable roles in which such performances are possible depend, in turn, crucially on her ability to maintain good and trustful relations with all countries, especially the leading bloc powers. Switzerland has its institutionalized role as the seat of many important international organizations. Sweden has established a position in international disarmament negotiations. Finland is still in search of a durable function in international peace politics. In this kind of analysis, Austria tends to fall somewhere between Finland on the one hand and Sweden and Switzerland on the other.

"Perhaps only Finland could render this significant political service without evoking conflicts at that point of time when the Central European political situation was still delicate." This assessment of the country's contribution as the catalyst of the CSCE process can be found in a recent authoritative book on Finland's foreign policy[14]. Of course, the Finns themselves may tend to exaggerate their innovative role in this context. I personally would prefer not to regard Finland's role as indispensable, because this would almost imply that the whole process which led to the signing of the CSCE Final Act depended on the success of a series of actions by a small peripheral nation. In other words, even if Finland had not been able to take the initiative and play the role of the catalyst and host State, some other neutral country, most likely Austria or Switzerland, could have been entrusted with those tasks. Sweden had disqualified herself at that time by her extremely heavy criticism of US actions in Vietnam. Nonetheless, the historical fact remains that this important role in the CSCE process was performed by Finland and that she was able to utilize successfully her good relations with all the countries concerned. As a side-effect, the international awareness of Finland's will and capacity to act neutrally in this kind of task was strengthened.

Since the Helsinki Summit, Finland's CSCE policy has been based on close coordination and cooperation with the other European neutral and non-aligned countries. In the present international situation, no major moves in connection with the CSCE can be expected from any State. Especially Finland is unlikely to take any major international initiatives in this context as long as East-West relations remain highly tense. Besides, a division of labor has been emerging within the "n+n"group, which means that Finland is going to get only a modest share of the future CSCE roles suitable for States which are not alliance members.

6. Finland's Role in European Image Politics

Since the late 1960s, Finland has unwillingly had to play a major international role in the "Finlandization" debate which has been going on in the Western world. The basic thesis, especially of those academic analysts who use this term, is that Finland has been losing her independence through a process of incrementally increasing submission to the Soviet Union, and that this might also happen to

Western Europe as a whole unless the nations of this region adopt a more intransigent and critical posture towards the Soviets[15]. To understand this debate, it is necessary to take into account the following historical facts:

— The talk about "Finlandization" began at the same time as the CSCE process was initiated.

— The "Finlandization" debate was at its liveliest in the mid-1970s, or up to the point when increasing East-West tensions began to replace the atmosphere of *détente* in Europe and in Superpower relations.

— There has been a continuous international discussion of the position of Western Europe *vis-à-vis* the USSR, particularly in the context of Atlantic relations, since the beginning of the "Cold War" in the late 1940s. Finland's position as a neighbor of the Soviet Union also attracted occasional attention in the West during Paasikivi's and the early years of Kekkonen's presidency. Sometimes Finland's position was perhaps even discussed in order to detect the true intentions behind Soviet foreign policy. However, there was no systematic international debate on Finland before the mid-1960s, and Finland's status was hardly ever used as a warning example for Western Europe in those years.

— The only major change in Finland's international position or foreign policy in the late 1960s was her increasingly active peace policy, especially in connection with the CSCE.

— Although the discussion about "Finlandization" is still under way, it has become more sporadic since the mid-1970s in a political climate of growing international tension.

These historical facts suggest two major conclusions: First, the "Finlandization" debate is not so much a Cold War as a *détente* discussion. In other words, Finland's assumed example has been used to oppose *détente* rather than to fuel the Cold War. Second, those who have employed the term "Finlandization" have not been so much interested in Finland's position as such, but rather in utilizing their own purposeful interpretations of it as a psychological instrument for wider purposes.

Perhaps the most comprehensive and detailed historical survey of the evidence of "Finlandization" in Western Europe is contained in the book "Soviet Foreign Policy toward Western Europe" edited by George Ginsburgs and Alvin Rubinstein. The editors seem to have tried to persuade the authors of the chapters of this book that Finland is thoroughly "Finlandized" in the negative sense of the term, and that Western Europe faces the immediate risk of "Finlandization". However, the individual contributions which deal with Finland, Austria, France, the Federal Republic of Germany and the United Kingdom all come to the conclusion that the signs of "Finlandization" in these countries including Finland are actually rather few.[16] Instead of getting involved in the complexities of the various possible interpretations of the historical facts of Finland's post-war international position, I shall say a few words on how the "Finlandization" debate has affected Finland and how she has tried to cope with the problems this debate has caused her.

Finland has virtually no possibilities to stifle talk of "Finlandization", simply because the discussion does not follow from what Finland is, says or does, but rather from the development of European politics in general, as I have tried to show above. However, Finland's responses to this debate may make a difference, because some reactions may be used by those who want to cultivate the term as an additional argument in support of their chosen theses. Especially if Finland reacts with loud and sharp protests, this may be interpreted as psychological evidence that there is something to those accusations. But if she fails to react, this may also be taken as an indication that she admits the validity of the claims that she is being "Finlandized".

Finland's actual response first tended to vacillate between silence and sharp counter-arguments, mainly within the conceptual framework provided by the debate itself. Then she tried to introduce a different meaning by maintaining that she was willing to accept the term if it was understood as peaceful and fruitful coexistence with the Soviet Union. This theme tended to dominate the Finnish reactions during the last years of Kekkonen's presidency. Under President Koivisto, a shift towards a more unconcerned or indifferent posture may be taking place, although it is too early to say anything definite in this respect yet[17].

The occasionally sharp Finnish reactions to talk of "Finlandization" can probably be explained partly by the fact that the political mentality of the nation, perhaps even the basic national character of the Finns, is rather sensitive to all foreign criticism. Part of the explanation may also lie in psychological miscalculations.

More important, however, is the fact that the success of the country's foreign policy as a whole is so vitally dependent on a favorable international image and goodwill that any international discussions in which her name is linked in a negative sense to the basic conflicts of the Great Powers or some current bloc-political campaign are bound to puzzle the Finnish foreign policy authorities. Such discussions may even objectively weaken her potential for contributing to European peace and security. This has hardly been the motive of anybody who has used the term "Finlandization", but it may be an unintended side-effect.

7. Summary and Conclusions

Finland has made her main contributions to European peace and security by stabilizing her own relations with the Soviet Union and by gaining international recognition of her neutrality. This has permitted her to establish and develop political, economic and cultural relations in all directions in accordance with the nation's international interests and national character. This contribution is likely to continue. As an undesired side-effect of her particular relations with the Soviet Union, Finland's name has been used negatively in European and East-West image politics. Finland's efforts to prevent this have been, and are likely to remain, fairly ineffective. In fact, Finland may now be adopting a more unconcerned attitude to this problem than before.

More specifically, Finland has consistently sought to promote Great Power disengagement and a nuclear freeze in the Nordic region. Although these efforts have thus far been rather unsuccessful, they may have indirectly contributed to the stabilization of Finland's international position, both as regards her relations with the Soviet Union and her position as a State practicing an active and peaceful policy of neutrality. Besides, Finland's initiatives may have significantly contributed to maintaining the factual non-nuclear status of the Nordic region. Finland's self-defined role as a "bridge-builder" between East and West has produced few concrete results—unless the country's international position as a whole is considered such a result. Finland's peace policy triumphed with the signing of the Final Act of the CSCE in Helsinki after many years of persistent but careful promotion of the positive factors for the conference that existed or were emerging in Great Power relations. The same role might have been performed by, for example, Austria, but the historical fact remains that it was played by Finland.

There are indications that Finland is adopting a modified, somewhat more flexible or responsive approach to Nordic security in the 1980s. Swedish cooperation or competition with Finland in the promotion of the idea of a Nordic nuclear-free zone may also change the Finnish role in this respect. Finland's role in the CSCE has radically diminished since 1975, and she is now more likely to continue her low-profile cooperation with the other members of the "n+n" group than to take new spectacular initiatives of her own.

One of the main problems of Finland's foreign policy is that she has not yet been able to establish any such durable or permanent role in European peacemaking which would automatically maintain and enhance the international recognition and prestige she has been able to acquire thus far by performing a few significant but temporary functions, such as being the catalyst and host of CSCE. In this respect, Finland's position is still less secure and strong than that of Switzerland, Sweden and Austria.

Notes

1 There is a lack of up-to-date comprehensive historical studies of Finland's post-war foreign policy in major Western languages. See, however, e. g. Raimo Väyrynen, Stability and Change in Finnish Foreign Policy (Helsinki 1972); Hans Peter Krosby, Friede für Europas Norden. Die sowjetisch-finnischen Beziehungen von 1944 bis zur Gegenwart (Wien, Düsseldorf 1981).
2 The term "security community" was introduced and applied to the Nordic region in Karl Deutsch, Political Community and the North Atlantic Area (Princeton, N. J., 1957).
3 For two illuminating analyses on intra-Nordic relations and the Nordic links to bloc politics see Krister Wahlbäck, The Nordic Region in Twentieth Century European Politics, and Nils Andrén, Changing Strategic Perspectives in Northern Europe, both in: Bengt Sundelius (ed.), Foreign Policies of Northern Europe (Boulder, Colorado, 1982).
4 The more restrained attitudes of the Scandinavian countries are perhaps to a large extent attributable to the failure of the plan for a Scandinavian defense alliance in the late 1940s.
5 Speech published in Maakansa, 23 January 1952.
6 The Finnish-Soviet communiqué on 25 November 1961. Ulkopoliittisia lausuntoja ja asiakirjoja 1961, pp. 1983.
7 For an analysis of the idea of Nordic nuclear-free zone as related to its wider international contexts see Osmo Apunen, Nuclear-Weapon-Free Areas, Zones of Peace and Nordic Security, 5 Yearbook of Finnish Foreign Policy (1978), pp. 2.
8 Speech by President Kekkonen on 29 November 1965, Ulkopoliittisia lausuntoja ja asiakirjoja 1965, pp. 31; statement by President Koivisto on 11 March 1983, Helsingin Sanomat 12 March 1983.
9 Harto Hakovirta, Koivisto's Presidency and the Question of Changes in Finland's Foreign Policy, 23 Österreichische Zeitschrift für Außenpolitik (1983), pp. 95, esp. 99—100.
10 Finland's "bridge-building" rhetoric during its most vivid phase has been shortly analyzed with reference to the relevant documents in: Katarina Brodin, Finland's Utrikespolitiska doktrin — En Inneallsanalys av Paasikivis och Kekkonens uttalanden aren 1944—1968 (Stockholm 1971).
11 See e. g. Harto Hakovirta, Neutral States in East-West Economic Cooperation, 18 Co-existence, (1981), pp. 95.
12 Ibidem, especially pp. 115.
13 I have discussed these points in some more detail in my article Finland in International Tension and Détente, in: Berter Heurlin (ed.), Norden og den internationale spaending (Copenhagen 1982), especially pp. 42
14 Juhani Suomi, 1970-luvun perintö, in: Juhani Suomi (ed.), Näkökulmia Suomen turvallisuuspolitiikkaan 1980-luvulla (Keuruu 1980), pp. 11, quotation from p. 13.
15 For a typical analysis stressing this theme, see Walter Laqueur, The Political Psychology of Appeasement — Finlandization and Other Unpopular Essays (New Brunswick, N. J., 1980), pp. 3; cf. George Maude, Has Finland been Finlandized? in: George Ginsburgs/Alvin Z. Rubinstein (eds.), Soviet Foreign Policy toward Western Europe (New York 1978), pp. 43.
16 Ibidem, passim.
17 Hakovirta, op. cit. (footnote 9), p. 101.

Nils Andrén

Swedish Institute of International Affairs, Stockholm

Sweden: Neutrality, Defense and Disarmament

1. Introduction

"We need disarmament in order to make the world safe for all countries, including ourselves"[1]

The main themes of this paper are the development and character of the Swedish policy of neutrality and its significance for Sweden's role in international disarmament and arms control efforts[2]. The underlying assumption for raising this issue is obviously that "neutral" States historically have had a distinct and useful function in these efforts and possibly can maintain and increase their importance in this respect if they can find effective methods of coordinating their intellectual and political endeavors.

The paper consists of two major parts. The first deals with neutrality, its background and conditions, the second with disarmament and arms control. After a) an introduction to some essential questions related to neutrality, the paper b) opens with a brief historical outline of Sweden's role as a neutral and not-aligned country. Special reference is made to c) problems raised by economic integration, d) defense and e) "active neutrality" and international "moralism".

In the second part Sweden's role in disarmament and arms control, and its conditions, are overviewed in sections on a) disarmament and arms control and b) Sweden and disarmament after World War II. The paper closes with c) an attempt to evaluate the factors influencing Sweden's disarmament behavior and with d) some questions raised and some tentative answers offered concerning Sweden's future role in the disarmament field.

2. Neutrality

a) The Essence of Neutrality

Surveying the countries of the world which claim the status of neutrals, it is obvious that they represent a wide variety of external conditions and policy responses. "Neutral" has, in wide circles, acquired as positive conceptual value; as all terms thus charged, it has been adopted for various political purposes, related both to external security and to domestic issues.

Hence an overview of Swedish "neutrality" should start with some basic definitions and clarifications. In international law, neutrality is related to a situation of war and refers to a State not participating in a war between other States. In international law, the neutral State has both obligations and rights. It is clear, however, that in the general discussion neutrality is also used as a term for describing an uncommitted stance between rival parties which are not necessarily involved in open hostilities, but have very conflicting interests and tense relations[3]. The post-war habit of describing a state of uneasy but stable peace as "Cold War" adds to the confusion. It even leads to the legally absurd claim to be neutral in peace—but not necessarily in war.

Sweden's basic definition of its international position in this respect is very simple and unambiguous. Sweden has adopted a *not*-aligned (to avoid the—possibly—politically misleading word *non*-aligned) position in peace-time with the firm intention of remaining neutral should there be a war in its environment. In view of its purpose, this policy of not-alignment may hence also be called a policy of neutrality, and indeed normally is. This policy is established by unilateral declaration; it is neither internationally guaranteed nor constitutionally prescribed.

A policy of neutrality leads already in peace-time to a number of restrictions and demands, in order to make the policy credible to the outside world in general and, in particular, to the powers which in case of a war may have a special strategic interest in the territory of the "neutral" country. Hence, the use of the term "neutral" in peace-time may be accepted as indicating the attitude of a State which intends to observe internationally prescribed or nationally perceived and declared conditions of neutrality for its pattern of behavior in war-time, and to adjust its peace-time behavior accordingly.

b) Sweden Neutral and Not-Aligned

Sweden's past as much as its present illustrates the importance of geopolitical or strategic conditions for the foreign policy options of a country. When the traditional Baltic powers, some four hundred years ago, were in a partly transient, partly permanent state of political disorder and dissolution, they left a power vacuum in which the rising Swedish kingdom (until 1809 also including Finland) could, in the 17th century, step in and establish itself as a major regional power. After less than a hundred years the conditions changed. Sweden's military power and political influence were greatly reduced, in relative as much as in absolute terms. The political and psychological adjustment to the change from greatness to weakness was a gradual and not wholly painless process. Eventually, after more than a century, a practically permanent policy of neutrality emerged. It was conditioned by Sweden's strategic location between mutually suspicious or openly rivaling Great Powers—whether the German Empire versus Czarist Russia (until 1918), Nazi Germany versus the Soviet Union or NATO versus the Warsaw Pact (or: the United States with Western Europe versus the Soviet Union and its East European "clients").

Somewhat paradoxically, the firmness of the Swedish attachment to a policy of neutrality is illustrated by the fact that it has never been tested in the official opinion polls dealing with questions of defense and security. It is always taken for granted, and nobody seems to object to this attitude.

It is hardly possible to single out the year or even the decade when Sweden definitely subscribed to its now traditional international principles. In 1890, King Oscar II spoke of Sweden's intention to be "neutral as far as possible, and even a bit further"[4]. During World War I the policy of neutrality was an axiom for Sweden — however, not quite for its warfaring neighbors[5]. Sweden has, ever since that time, proclaimed a policy of neutrality in all open conflicts between Great Powers. Given the fact that this policy has helped Sweden to stay out of all European wars (Sweden has indeed not participated as a belligerent in a war since the era of Napoleon I) the policy could be called an unqualified success. Some caution is, however, justified: The policy of neutrality was a necessary, but not a sufficient condition. In difficult situations, especially during World War II, Sweden was probably also protected by other conditions, mainly outside its direct influence[6].

The call for broader international solidarity, leading to the formation in 1919 of the League of Nations and in 1945 to the establishment of the United Nations, raised some new problems for neutral countries. Switzerland solved them by being granted exemption from obligations in respect of military sanctions in the League and, so far, by abstaining from membership in the United Nations—but willingly hosting, wholly or in part, both organizations. In Sweden, the lack of universality, especially of the League, and the rules on sanctions of both organizations caused serious worries. As for the League, the fact that military sanctions—except the transit of League troops through the territories of member States—were not compulsory reduced the obligations to harmless proportions for a neutral State. As the dissolution of the League progressed, Sweden, along with other small States, terminated its sanction obligations by unilateral declaration. The

United Nations posed, in principle, a more difficult problem; here compulsory sanctions included also military measures. By becoming a member Sweden might, at least in theory, be drawn into a conflict. However, in practice, the veto power of the rivaling Great Powers in the Security Council removed completely the possibility of decisions on sanctions that might compel member States to participate in an armed conflict between Great Powers[7].

Sweden demonstrated its awareness of the practical compatibility between UN membership and virtual neutrality by observing that if "against expectation" the United Nations tended to split into two camps, Sweden would not allow itself to be drawn into a group or bloc formation[8]. This marginal observation was soon to be transformed into a firm policy declaration.

A new warning came in connection with the proclamation of the Marshall Plan (1947). Sweden declared, in its own economic interest, that it perceived it as a reconstruction plan, not as the formation of a bloc directed against outside powers. This was clearly not the interpretation of the Soviet Union, and hardly in full conformity with the political intentions behind the Plan. However, the situation made Sweden refine the definition of its declaration of bloc-independence: Sweden would not choose sides by "affiliating with a great power bloc, neither by an express alliance treaty, nor by tacit understanding on common military measures in case of a conflict"[9].

The final moment of decision came when the conditional fears expressed by the Swedish government became obvious facts. In 1948, the Brussels Pact was concluded by West European States as an instrument of protection, not against a resurging German threat, but against the Soviet war ally. The alarm bell was the Soviet take-over in Czechoslovakia. A year later, the Atlantic Pact was forged as an American effort to protect an ailing Europe against what many Western political leaders with broad popular support perceived as an imminent Soviet threat.

Sweden's reaction to the emergence of the „Cold War" revealed a variety of ambitions and fears. The World War II experience of Great Power presence, intervention and war was still fresh. To maintain Sweden's own policy of neutrality and to protect Sweden's immediate environment from involvement in the power bloc confrontation became two obvious Swedish goals. There was, at least in theory, one way of attaining both of them. The solution chosen by the Swedish government—with broad opposition support—could, however, also be interpreted as an infringement of the policy of neutrality, as it would mean a commitment undertaken in advance to fight for other countries. It was formulated in a Swedish offer to Norway and Denmark to establish a Scandinavian defense alliance. The condition was that the member States should all commit themselves to conducting a policy of neutrality, basically according to the Swedish model. Finland had recently concluded its Treaty of Friendship, Co-operation and Mutual Assistance with the Soviet Union (1948) and could not be included in a Scandinavian arrangement. A defense alliance should, however, also have been in the Finnish interest. By preventing direct NATO involvement in any of the Scandinavian countries, the alliance could well have alleviated Soviet fears[10].

The Swedish plan failed; for the Norwegians the World War II experience finally proved stronger than the still forceful undercurrent of traditional "neutralism". Hence they would not accept the requirement of total neutrality. Denmark, with some expressions of reluctance, followed Norway in early 1949 into the new Western alliance. Sweden was never tempted to follow the example of the two West Scandinavian States[11]. The logic of both the historical experience and the strategic situation was overwhelming.

The aim of the Swedish initiative to form a Scandinavian defense alliance was to obviate a threatening deterioration—caused by increasing Great Power involvement—in Sweden's security environment as a not-aligned country. Keeping this goal in mind, the failure of the Scandinavian alliance also proved for a very long time at least a partial success. It facilitated the acceptance of conditions—the refusal to allow foreign NATO forces to be permanently stationed and nuclear weapons to be deployed on their territories in peace-time—for Denmark's and Norway's membership in the Atlantic Alliance[12]. It also contributed to the conditions for Finland's successful development of its post-war relations with the Soviet Union: avoiding membership of the Warsaw Pact (in 1955), retaining a democratic system and also joining the "Nordic Commonwealth", which—with the Nordic Council as its pivotal institution—developed as a political, economic, social and cultural factor. It expanded, both in spite of, and as a defensive reaction to the different Nordic roads to national security[13].

In this way the Swedish policy of neutrality adjusted itself to the new situation from the end of World War II to the formation of the divisive pact systems. The policy of neutrality was reaffirmed with the new formula of "not-alignment between power blocs", from which the special reference to power blocs was gradually omitted as the memory of Sweden's own efforts to form a "bloc"—albeit a minor and neutral one—waned.

But there were other problems ahead, connected with Sweden's role as a committed democratic State, deeply involved in the rapidly expanding market economies, not only in Europe. Some of these issues would remind the Swedes of the limits of their country's international options which might be imposed by the concern for a credible security policy. Another problem was related to the defense of a small, not-aligned country between heavily armed, nuclear power blocs.

c) The Importance of Economic Integration

The most important question, apart from security—to be aligned or not-aligned, to be defended by others also or to rely on self-defense only—was economic cooperation. Here also, attempts were made to promote regional, Nordic solutions. Several steps were taken especially to facilitate the movement of labor in the Nordic area. In the 1950s, a painstaking investigation of the conditions of a future Nordic market was carried out, with the purpose of providing the basis for political decisions to transform the Nordic countries into a "common market". The proposal, behind which Sweden, supported by Denmark, was the driving force, suffered, however, in 1958 the same fate as the project of a Scandinavian defensive alliance had earlier, and for a similar reason: Norway did not regard itself as—yet—sufficiently strong to match Swedish and Danish competition. A Nordic market was, however, realized a few years later, in an indirect way. All the Nordic countries joined EFTA[14], together with Austria, Great Britain, Portugal and Switzerland, preferring a European free trade area to the more ambitions scheme represented by EEC.

For Sweden, EFTA was a favorable solution: it enabled Sweden to participate in expanding economic integration without prejudicing the credibility of its security policy. However, when Great Britain in 1961 decided to apply for EEC membership, Sweden was suddenly faced with the problem of whether it should follow suit—for which there were many sound economic reasons—or decide that EEC membership was incompatible with credible not-alignment. Sweden was not prepared to apply for membership[15]; in fact, it is doubtful whether at that time it had a real option. As General de Gaulle declared the British not to be good enough as Europeans, Sweden's final decision could be postponed for almost a decade. However, when the issue became real the Swedish position was basically the same, although the arguments were rephrased in reaction to perceived long-term effects of the Werner and Davignon plans[16]. Full membership in an organization like EEC, with supranational powers and declared ambitions for their further development and, also, with all members (before Ireland's entry) belonging to NATO, was not in the Swedish interest.

Nevertheless, a solution had to be found in order to protect, as far as possible, Sweden's economic interests, without prejudicing the credibility of its security policy. Like Norway—and eventually also Finland—Sweden settled its relations with the Common Market in a free trade agreement, which after some ten years should put the major part of Swedish-EEC trade on equal conditions with intra-EEC trade. Thus Sweden tried to combine the blessings of economic integration with the compelling need for political integrity as a not-aligned State. The price was economic integration without formal power in the EEC system[17].

Norway had refused membership, after a referendum, for clearly domestic reasons. For Finland, the restrictions inherent in its strategic position were prohibitive, while Sweden, using the external factor as the exclusively decisive explanation, in fact also avoided domestic difficulties (especially in the Social Democratic Party) by rejection of formal EEC membership.

d) The Significance of Defense

The Swedish policy of neutrality has always assumed the need for an adequate national defense, strong enough to deter and, if necessary, turn back any violator of Swedish territory. This is not the place to argue whether this aim has been or is likely to be adequately achieved. Recent and widely broadcast activities under the surface of Sweden's territorial waters have—to say the least—clearly illustrated the difficulties with which Sweden has to deal[18].

The feeling—well-founded or not—that a stronger defense could have saved Sweden from humiliating deviations from the principles of neutrality and other problems during and after World War II has clearly been an important factor behind Swedish defense policy[19].

Any small country—and especially one with a large territory and a small population—is often confronted, both at home and abroad, with questions concerning feasibility and credibility. Countries belonging to this category should in all honesty be ready to concede that situations may arise where the means may not equal the ambitions. Most countries are, however,also likely to have developed a philosophy or a set of political and strategic doctrines enhancing the possibility and plausibility of realizing their security goals. In Sweden, these goals are summed up in the above-mentioned formula: not-alignment in peace in order to ensure neutrality in war. The set of principles formulated in Sweden for this purpose may briefly be summarized as follows:

—It is assumed that military threats against Sweden can primarily, and perhaps only, arise as a result of the rivalries between the two power blocs in Europe.

—Should any power or bloc contemplate an attack against Sweden, it is unlikely that the aggressor would be able and willing to use more than a marginal fraction of its total military resources against Sweden.

—If an aggressor can only use a minor part of its resources, the demands that Swedish defense must meet in order to be effectively "dissuading" (or "deterring") should not be insurmountable.

—An isolated nuclear attack is not regarded as a credible scenario. A nuclear attack against Sweden as an extension of a nuclear war in Europe is also regarded as implausible; should a war in Europa go nuclear, it is likely to be too short and too destructive to make any flank operation meaningful. The greatest nuclear threat would arise if a war escalated to the nuclear level only after Sweden had been subjected to a conventional attack. This scenario is thought to underline the importance of a national defense strong enough to dissuade a conventional aggression. Otherwise, the side-effects of a major nuclear war outside Sweden are regarded as the primary nuclear civil defense scenario.

—There is also a doctrine of economic self-reliance as an important instrument to sustain a credible policy of neutrality[20].

One important aspect of this principle of self-reliance is related to defense-oriented research, development and production of war material. In Sweden—as in many other countries—the World War II years represented a major breakthrough for close cooperation between scientific research and industrial development concerning a wide range of instruments for warfare. A parliamentary decision in 1944 led to the amalgamation of various research efforts into a National Defense Research Institute, with a staff, at the peak of its post-war development, of some 1,500, working on all major aspects of defense research, including, until the mid 1960s, basic research related to the development of nuclear weapons[21].

At present, Sweden's defense forces suffer from the economic crisis like the rest of the Swedish society. Ambitions which previously were self-evident have had to be reduced. At the same time, Sweden has been exposed to—or just become aware of?—a new type of threat, represented by peace-time violations of Swedish territorial waters by foreign submarines. This has contributed to domestic debate and foreign—especially Soviet—criticism and doubt of the general credibility of Sweden's security policy[22].

e) Active Neutrality and International Moralism

The idea that a not-aligned, democratic welfare State would, already by its existence, make a useful international contribution—or even serve as a model[23]—is related to two important themes of the Swedish policy of neutrality. A not-aligned State would, by virtue of its independent position, be able to perform useful functions in the international system. Not only Dag Hammarskjöld, as the second UN Secretary-General, and a number of other high international officials, but also Swedish contingents which participated in UN peace-keeping activities have served as illustrations supporting this view. A second point has more immediate relevance for the disarmament issue, namely the performance of an active role in international negotiations. This role has at times been assigned an importance great enough to influence Sweden's international behavior in important respects. Its usefulness in this role has depended on its ability to abstain from engaging itself in the political struggle between East and West. At times the question has been raised whether this "self-control" also had to include ideological neutrality. Even if Sweden's actual behavior in this respect has never been absolutely consistent, the principle of ideological neutrality has always been firmly rejected[24].

When the idea of an "active neutrality", as a peace-time policy, was approved and adopted by a number of "neutral" countries, Sweden could already look back on various contributions and efforts in support of international cooperation and organizations. The rejection of ideological neutrality pointed to another option for international activity—with old roots in Sweden's political culture: to take sides emotionally and even assume the pretentious role of a moral arbiter on various international issues[25]. Clearly, the ambition has always been to do so without prejudice to the principle of not-alignment and the credibility as a prospective neutral. However, it has not been possible to avoid criticism to the effect that the basic security policy goals are put in jeopardy.

The Swedish diplomat Sverker Aström has raised a question of principle: "Do we act at variance with the prime purpose of our policy by exercising this right", *inter alia,* "to criticize phenomena that are contrary to our democratic principles and to basic human rights, to demand respect for international law and for the interests of the small nations?" Aström rejects the idea that this aspect of "active neutrality" involves any security risks. On the basis of historical experience he assumes "that even strong declarations by a neutral country, based on principle and ideology, are not in themselves causes of military attack against that country"[26].

This does not exclude that such attitudes can be used as a pretext for actions, should other motives warrant them—and even facilitate a decision. Nor do they exclude diplomatic pressures and punishment, and other negative effects—as Sweden experienced during the Vietnam conflict. "Active neutrality" of this kind can also raise other problems. If the moral and other reactions tend to focus more on conditions in distant countries than on the situation in the immediate vicinity, this may breed complex and predominantly negative reactions, and indeed already has: "The foreign policy debate in... Sweden is to a great extent moving on the level of dreams and hopes, or of intellectual dishonesty and hypocrisy"[27].

3. Disarmament

a) Disarmament and Arms Control

In principle, neutral countries hold a unique position on disarmament and arms control. Uncommitted to any power bloc interest, they are, again in principle, able to take a more detached view, at times revealing unpleasant truths and at times helping in finding solutions, at best to break a dead-lock, at least to avoid the collapse of international negotiations on disarmament and arms control. It would, however, be a gross exaggeration to assume that the role of the "neutrals" in this process is completely void of any self-interest. Nevertheless, this does not seriously reduce their special position. As small and "neutral" States, their self-interests often tend to coincide, to a large degree, with what we may call the interest of the whole international system, or rather of international order. For all small States in general and for those that are unprotected by major powers and alliances in particular, a peaceful development of the international system, enhancing the role and rule of international law, is a primary interest. A reduction of tensions between major powers is also clearly in the interest of small States[28].

In one particular sense, in the nuclear age, the difference between big and small, powerful and weak, offensive and defensive States is probably reduced: All share the basic ambition of national and human survival. This ambition is clearly containing other national ambitions or, at least, influencing the choice of the methods to achieve them. However, both for domestic and alliance-client purposes, major powers find it also necessary to play games—dangerous as they may seem, or perhaps are—in which tension and *détente,* armaments and arms reductions, and even peace and war, may be the stakes.

Small and "neutral" States are neither politically self-effacing nor lacking any national goals of their own[29]. But it is also an exaggeration to maintain or pretend that the hope of reducing the strength of a future aggressor against Sweden is a leading motive, if a motive at all, when the Swedes participate in disarmament negotiations in the international fora to which they, in spite of being both a small and not-aligned country, have aquired access.

Swedish disarmament negotiators have maintained that successful arms reduction negotiations have as an unconditional prerequisite that they do not change the power balance between the parties involved[30]. Clearly much of the difficulties in past and present arms reduction talks are due to the avowed or suspected intention to change the present military power balance. "Reassurance" and "deterrence" apply to arms control as much as to arms races[31].

Arms reductions may have direct significance for Sweden also. We have noted that Sweden's defense doctrines are based on the assumption that the balance between the power blocs makes it unlikely that an aggressor will have very large forces available for operations against a marginal target like Sweden. The conclusion is obvious: It should be in Sweden's interest that the balance on which the marginal usefulness of Swedish defense is based not be seriously upset, even by negotiated arms reductions. It is, however, open to question how dominant this aspect has been as a Swedish concern during arms reduction negotiations[32].

To a broker-minded participant like Sweden, an overriding problem may often rather be to help the Superpowers to agree on anything at all. The dialogue itself assumes an importance of its own, and significant disarmament or arms control measures recede as a distant aim or only a theoretical goal. Even ill-tempered negotiations may be better than silent lack of contact: If dogs do not bark, they might bite[33].

There are several aspects of disarmament. The post-war negotiations have dealt with the reduction and limitation of certain classes of weapons, especially nuclear weapons (test-ban and non-proliferation treaties, SALT, START and INF). The Geneva conferences of the United Nations, under different titles and acronyms, and with growing participation, have dealt since 1962 with a broad variety of issues, not only the original task of "general and complete disarmament" but also with special tasks related to nuclear weapons, chemical weapons and weapons of mass destruction. In Vienna, the eternal dialogue—or exchange of monologues—on M(B)FR has been going on since 1973. The series of conferences on security and cooperation in Europe—in Geneva, Helsinki, Belgrade and Madrid, with the Stockholm conference in 1984 as an offspring, have the difficult issue of confidence building measures as a controversial theme. Finally, there are also the "diplomatic conferences", dealing with unusually cruel or inhumane weapons.

The Swedish disarmament policies reflect, as much as do the defense policies, the state of the outside world and the expectations and fears for the future. During the years between the World Wars, the strategic vacuum, which emerged in the Baltic area with the defeat of the two leading Great Powers in the region, encouraged a strong current of unilateralism in the Swedish approach to disarmament. It was caused, *inter alia,* by a mix of hopes and lack of understanding of the forces at work in the European system, and internal political considerations, leading to what may, with some oversimplification, be described as "a somewhat naive attempt" to influence other States by setting a good example[34].

We have already noted the influence of the European crises in the mid-1930s and World War II on Swedish defense policy. The unilateralism of the 1920s did not return as an open political force; it has remained, however, as a "pacifist" undercurrent, intermittently boiling up to the surface. It has, at times, been reinforced by the argument that Sweden should set an example for the world, indeed that the Swedish type or level of defense preparations was a threat to Sweden's credibility as an actor in disarmament negotiations. The official attitude, clearly supported by a strong majority of public opinion, reacts strongly against this view. The idea of incompatibility between Sweden's defense and disarmament policies is firmly denied. "Sweden's active work for international disarmament is part of the Swedish security policy in a wide sense: We need disarmament in order to make the world safer for all nations, including ourselves." But Swedish defense remains necessary "so long as the leading nuclear powers maintain large standing forces in our neighborhood." The chief responsibility for the success of disarmament must remain with the Superpowers[35].

b) Sweden and Disarmament after World War II

It has been noted that Sweden's activities in the field of disarmament remained at a low level during the first phase of the post-war period[36]. This may in part be ascribed to the war experiences and the impact of the "Cold War", to which the Swedish response was not-alignment and resolute armament. Another important factor was that international disarmament activities hardly existed outside the futile Superpower dialogue on nuclear weapons. It should also be kept in mind that during the 1950s the dominating nuclear issue in Sweden was not how to abolish the Superpower weapons but whether or not Sweden should nuclearize its defense[37].

It is, however, also obvious that Sweden expected the new World Organization to have as one of its most important tasks "an organized and systematic limitation of armament[38]." It has been observed that Sweden did not raise the disarmament issue in the United Nations until 1955. On the whole, Sweden seems to have followed the UN majority on issues related to disarmament. The memory of the frustrating disarmament conferences between the Wars also made Swedish delegates weary of calls for global disarmament conferences. Also, in the early years of the United Nations, proposals concerning disarmament were too closely related to the "Cold War" to have any attraction for "neutral" countries[39].

Nuclear weapons were regarded as the key to the disarmament problem, and they also became the object of the first major Swedish international initiative in the field. The Swedish Foreign Minister (Östen Undén) raised the test ban issue—to become a major Swedish preoccupation in years to come—and the question of regional zones, where not only nuclear weapons should be banned, but also restrictions applied to conventional armaments[40]. Sweden's mounting active concern about disarmament was also reflected in a demand that the Ten Power Committee on Disarmament, set up by the United Nations, should be reorganized to include other States as well. Sweden's goal to be admitted to such a new forum was attained in 1962, when the Committee was enlarged and reformed as the Eighteen Nations Disarmament Conference (ENDC) in Geneva.

A much-noted Swedish proposal was submitted in 1961, when Undén introduced his idea of a "club" of non-nuclear States. Such a "club" was to exert moral pressure on the Great Powers by not only refusing to produce nuclear weapons but also by not allowing the deployment of nuclear weapons on the territory of its members. Reference to the Undén Plan has often been made in connection with later proposals for nuclear-free zones; in fact, the "club" was not conceived as a regional arrangement. The main support for the plan came from the Eastern bloc and the "Third World", while NATO—with the exception of its Nordic members—opposed it. For NATO, the possibility of deploying nuclear arms on the territory of non-nuclear allies was as unnegotiable in 1961 as some 20 years later[41].

Irrespective of the original intentions, the "club" idea resulted in a demarcation of Sweden's position between the power blocs by challenging NATO interests. If this had been the intention—a doubtful proposition which would be difficult to substantiate—, it could also have been understood as a move balancing Undén's earlier blunt and much praised rejection of the Soviet idea of transforming the Baltic into a "Sea of Peace"[42].

In a sense, the 1960s and early 1970s were the period of grand illusions for Sweden's disarmament policy. It is difficult to say whether the intensive Swedish activities in this field were the result of a deliberate new policy or of the anger and genius of Sweden's chief negotiators in the ENDC-CCD-CD conferences (Alva Myrdal 1962—1973 and Inga Thorson 1974—1982). The present writer is inclined to believe in the second interpretation. Naively high expectations at the outset ended in more realistic and mature disillusion, based on a better understanding of the character of Great Power politics and the "lack of good will" on both sides. In particular, the failure of the nuclear powers to match the undertakings of the nuclear "have-nots" in the Non-Proliferation Treaty by commitments to a total test ban and nuclear arms reductions caused strong reaction and bitterness[43].

In retrospect, Sweden's most important contribution may well be the idea of a seismic detection "club" with a purpose of registering all underground nuclear detonations. Sweden contributed to the realization of this idea by building, in 1968, a seismic observatory and publishing and distributing reports of its observations[44].

This is not the place for a full catalogue and analysis of all major and minor Swedish initiatives and attitudes in disarmament and arms control questions. The main emphasis during the whole period has remained on nuclear weapons; a special concern has been to support the perception of a high nuclear threshold. The fear, in the early 1970s, that "mini-nukes" would blur the difference between conventional and nuclear weapons can be seen in this context.

The main interest in the field of conventional weapons has centered on the efforts to outlaw particularly "inhumane weapons". It should also be noted that Sweden has taken an active and innovative interest in negotiations on biological and chemical weapons and methods of non-penetrating supervision of arms control measures[45].

Sweden's desire to strengthen the organizational disarmament structure achieved notable success when the UN Disarmament Division was gradually elevated to become the UN Department of Disarmament (successively headed by two Swedes)[46].

In the 1970s, Sweden's major initiatives in the United Nations on issues related to disarmament focussed on background studies of basic importance, hopefully with long-term effects but with little practical impact in a shorter perspective. Mention should be made both of a proposal—submitted jointly with Sweden's three neighboring Nordic countries—for a UN study on the connection between disarmament and economic development (the proposal was adopted in 1977) and on nuclear weapons (in 1978).

In general, these brief observations on Sweden's disarmament activities have indicated that the efforts have been concentrated on long-term measures in order to influence the larger international environment, without specific attempts to promote more narrowly perceived Swedish national interests. The most recent efforts have only partly had a similar character, and they have been more directly related to a shorter perspective. The Swedish-Mexican proposal for a nuclear freeze moved into the highly controversial area of the Superpower INF negotiations by raising a related proposal on the UN agenda. The Palme Commission—although not a Swedish initiative—belongs also, already due to its leadership, to this context. Its proposal for ridding a zone in Central Europe of tactical nuclear weapons has been taken up by the Swedish government and submitted to other governments for their opinion—so far with very little success.

All these more recent activities are clearly related to the fears of nuclear war which have been resurging in recent years. The same judgment applies to the new—and in a historical perspective surprising—Swedish activities for establishing a nuclear-free zone in Northern Europe. It is hardly clear what such a zone would mean in practice; the Swedish concept has been defined in broad terms but it has not received the support of the other countries involved. The Nordic NATO members find it irreconcilable with their alliance undertakings. Even in Finland, which first raised the zone idea in a Nordic context (the "Kekkonen Plans") and still firmly supports the idea, it has also been observed that at present the plans for such a zone are hardly feasible[47].

Irrespective of the future of the zone proposals, they represent in principle a new departure in Swedish security policy. Certainly, they do not change the fact that the Swedish policy of neutrality is based on unilateral undertakings, rejecting all ideas of foreign "protection" by means of international agreements on neutralization (according to the Swiss model) or similar arrangements. However, in order to be meaningful, the establishment of a non-nuclear zone would have to involve the major powers. They might have to restrict deployment on their own territories and enter into some kind of agreement on a guaranteed "no-use" in return for the undertakings of the non-nuclear parties. The nuclear powers would have to give promises which would—implicitly or explicitly—be conditional. They would be valid as long as the countries in the non-nuclear zone remained non-nuclear. A crucial question is how a mechanism to control compliance with the conditions could be arranged without interfering with the integrity of a State, especially if not-aligned and neutral by unilateral declaration.

c) Some Conclusions

It is hardly an exaggeration to say that Sweden has exerted a greater influence in (and sometimes, perhaps, on) international disarmament deliberations and negotiations than is warranted by its size. It might be added that this observation does not apply to disarmament and arms control issues only. It was a fact long before armament came into focus that Sweden had established a reputation not only for disinterested efforts towards "objectivity" but also for its competence based on solid homework on international issues. This general image—acquired already during the League years—has certainly been important.

The policy of neutrality and not-alignment is clearly a key factor in this context. By virtue of its independence of alliance ties with the Superpowers and power blocs, Sweden has often been able to rally support for its proposals, especially among "n + n" and developing countries. Sweden's by-and-large non-colonial past is also likely to have been an asset in relation to the "new" States.

Oddly enough—or perhaps not so oddly—Sweden's defense policy, which was remarkably ambitious during some 20 years after World War II, has also constituted a very important asset in the disarmament context. It has helped Sweden to acquire and store a great amount of scientific and technological knowledge in fields of military importance. The National Defense Research Institute has been pointed out as particularly important in this context. The high level of scientific and military expert competence at the disposal of Swedish negotiators has enabled them to present alternative proposals, to subject the Superpower proposals to close expert scrutiny, and sometimes to call a bluff.

d) Which Role in the Future?

The role of a small actor in the disarmament game—however active and ambitious—depends on a number of factors. Some of them have been elaborated on in the previous sections. They include partly factors on which the actor concerned can wield a decisive influence:

- the goals of the actor;
- the means at his disposal;
- the competence of his negotiators and experts;
- the intensity of his interest in pursuing his goals.

The major factors deciding the role of the small actor in all international games—including disarmament and arms control—are, however, normally beyond the actor's control. They are closely related to the larger "scenario", including the general state of the international system, to the goals and interests of the major powers and not least to the actual readiness of the biggest actors—the

Superpowers—to work for tangible disarmament results, beyond such general phrases as "to achieve a stable balance at a reduced level of nuclear arsenals"[48] or to stand for "equality in nuclear and other armaments, for abstention from military supremacy"[49].

We have noted Swedish criticisms of the major powers for lack of seriousness of purpose regarding disarmament and arms control issues. In a practical disarmament perspective, this unwillingness—perceived or real—is an important fact. However, more than to criticize, it is important to understand the reasons behind the reluctance to engage in serious negotiations, such as mutual suspicion or political ambitions which are irreconcilable with arms reductions.

When negative factors of these kinds are operating, technical or formal difficulties—whether diplomatic or technological—rather serve as excuses for a policy governed by other considerations. For a country like Sweden (in which the fact-finding commission has almost from time immemorial been a national institution), with a high competence in defense technology, it has been natural to approach arms control with factual analysis.

With this approach, success, however limited it may be, depends on whether the real issues are related to the problems dealt with in such an analysis—or at least on whether the parties concerned are willing to pretend that they are. However, when the real issues—the political interests of the major powers—are thought to be negatively affected by disarmament measures technically within reach, the possibilities for progress and success by technical analysis and proposals are strictly limited and unlikely to yield more than hardly face-saving, token concessions.

As long as Sweden retains a high diplomatic and technological competence, and as long as it can maintain a political balance between the two power blocs (sustained by a credible national defense), two lines of action on disarmament and arms control issues seem to be available.

One is to follow the traditional approach in the negotiations: to use its diplomatic and technological proficiency in order to help the major parties to find solutions, while at the same time observing the restrictions that ought to be imposed for reasons of national security and making independent contributions whenever desirable and possible (such as the Swedish seismic observatory monitoring earthquakes and nuclear underground tests).

The other is to rely heavily on the political prestige created by independence between the power blocs and assume a leading role in building up political/public opinion "n + n" pressure against the dominating nuclear powers.

The first method aims at influencing, indeed convincing, the major powers by rational arguments. It is governed by many conditions, including access to the relevant international fora, discretion—low profile—and high competence. The main condition for the second method is that Sweden be regarded by other "n + n" States and their potential supporters in international organizations as genuinely uncommitted. Its purpose is more persuasion by political pressure than by rational arguments. Its public profile is often high and outspoken.

A third possibility would of course be to abandon the ambitions to influence the major powers and the international system, and simply try to protect narrow or limited national interests. While this element cannot be completely neglected, it has never been a major goal in Swedish disarmament policy—and is unlikely to be in the future[50].

To many politicians and analysts, the activities of Sweden in the field of disarmament and arms control traditionally stand out as very important. To others its present and future significance, as much as the impact that Sweden and other small States can make, may remain more doubtful. One fundamental question is whether disarmament—also when balanced and general—will have negative consequences for the national security or any other dominant national interest. It has also to do with the character of the international system and especially with its subdivision into "open" and "closed" political societies. When arguments have access easily—or at all—to the public only in countries with open political systems, there is a clear danger that public pressure for disarmament will eventually only influence the "open" camp and lead to a distortion of the international balance. These are well-known fears; they seem likely to make the second method, especially when combined with campaigns to mobilize the general public, unlikely to be successful.

These observations indicate a number of theoretical options, available to all actors in the game of disarmament. They are summarized in the following matrix.

Goals[51] / Methods	National security oriented	International system oriented
Technical approaches (expertise)		
Political approaches (brokerage or pressure)		

The options are characterized as theoretical as they can hardly be realized in any "pure" form. The practical options are always a mix—in varying proportions and indefinite numbers.

Notes

1 Karin Söder (Foreign Minister 1976—1978), in an address to "Svensk folkriksdag för nedrustning" (Swedish People's Parliament for Disarmament), 13 January, 1978. Documents of Swedish Foreign Policy, 1978, pp. 214 (Annual publication since 1950 by the Royal Ministry for Foreign Affairs, Stockholm, subsequently quoted as Documents + year.)

2 The terminology, including such terms as disarmament, arms reductions and arms control, reflects partly different ambitions. In this paper the terms are used without specific reference to these distinctions; the normal term here is "disarmament" or "disarmament and arms control".

3 Cf. Harto Hakovirta, Neutral States and Bloc-Based Integration, 13 Cooperation and Conflict (1978), pp. 109; idem, The Soviet Union and the Varieties of Neutrality in Western Europe. 35 World Politics (1982/83), pp. 563.

4 Quoted by Folke Lindberg, Den svenska utrikespolitikens historia (A History of Swedish Foreign Policy, vol. 3: 1872—1914, Stockholm 1958), p. 82.

5 There were both Russian fears and German expectations. Cf. Torsten Gihl, Den svenska utrikes-politikens historia (A History of Swedish Foreign Policy, vol. 4: 1914—1919; Stockholm 1951), pp. 29.

6 During the critical years 1939—1941 — when the German-Soviet Treaty was in effect — neither party would have accepted that the other acquire control of Sweden.

7 Art 27 (3) of the UN Charter. At the outbreak of the Korean conflict (in 1950) the absence of the Soviet Union enabled the Security Council to adopt a recommendation on military measures against North Korea, creating a dilemma for Sweden. Sweden showed her solidarity by supplying a field hospital and safeguarded her basic principles by issuing a declaration that the support of the United Nations was not an abandonment of her not-alignment in relation to the power blocs. Cf. Nils Andrén, Power-Balance and Non-Alignment: A Perspective on Swedish Foreign Policy (Stockholm 1967), pp. 73; also Royal Ministry of Foreign Affairs (ed.), Documents of Swedish Foreign Policy, 1950—1951 (Stockholm 1957).

8 Nils Andrén, op. cit., p. 40.

9 Ibid., p. 54.

10 The Scandinavian defense alliance project has been discussed and analyzed in a number of studies. For bibliographies see Johan Jørgen Holst (ed.), Five Roads to Nordic Security (Oslo 1972); Barbara Haskel, The Scandinavian Option: Opportunities and Opportunity Costs in Postwar Scandinavian Foreign Policies (Oslo 1976); and Bengt Sundelius (ed.), Foreign Policies of Northern Europe (Boulder, Colorado 1982).

11 Although some leading newspapers, notably Dagens Nyheter and Goeteborgs Handels- och Sjoefartstidning, supported by some odd politicians, opened an intensive pro-NATO campaign, the Western option was never considered.

12 Cf. references in note 10 and also Nils Andrén et al., The Future of the Nordic Balance (Stockholm 1977).

13 Nils Andrén, Nordic Integration, 3 Cooperation and Conflict (1967), pp. 1; Frantz Wendt, Cooperation in the Nordic Countries: Achievements and Obstacles (Stockholm 1981).

14 Finland did so by the formal establishment of a special instrument of cooperation between EFTA and Finland called FINEFTA.

15 The Swedish case was elaborated by the Prime Minister (Erlander) in a speech at the Metal Workers Annual Conference in 1961. Documents 1961. Also Andrén, op. cit. (note 7), pp. 124.

16 The main problem was the Davignon Plan on political unity. Swedish government memorandum, 18 March 1971. Documents 1971. Also Holst (ed.), op. cit., pp. 212.

17 The Swedish ambition was to establish and develop "as wide a cooperation as possible with due regard to our neutrality". Documents 1971.

18 Notably the „Whiskey on the Rocks" incident — the Soviet submarine in the restricted military area in the Karlskrona Archipelago, in 1981, and the „big hunt" a year later at the gates of the main naval base at Muskö.

19 The experiences during World War II were for a long time absolutely decisive. These have been analyzed in the "SUAV"-Project initiated by Stockholm historians on "Sweden during World War II" (Sverige under andra världskriget).

20 These doctrines have been steadily repeated in commission reports and memoranda, especially since Sweden in the 1960s officially abandoned the idea of acquiring nuclear weapons. Cf. also Nils Andrén, Swedish Defence Doctrines and Changing Threat Perspectives, 17 Cooperation and Conflict (1982), pp. 29.

21 Cf. further 1969 ars försvarsforskningsutredning (1969 Commission on Defense Research) and the report 1981 Lars försvarsforskningsstudie (1981 Defense Research Study) on the aims, conditions, and structures of defense research.

22 Cf. *inter alia* Ingmar Oldberg, En liten, nyttig kapitaliststat (A Small, Useful Capitalist State), in: Krigsvetenskapsakademiens Handlingar och Tidskrift (1982), pp. and Sovjetunionens syn pa Norden (The Soviet View of Northern Europe), in: Bidrag till Öststatsforskningen (Uppsala 1984).

23 E. g. Documents 1950—1951, pp. 14—15. At this time the Swedish government professed its belief that a democratic development like that of Sweden could „hardly fail in the long run to influence ideas, even in countries under ›the dictatorship of the proletariat‹."

24 In 1949 the government criticized the „usual misconception in that a neutrality programme means a duty to observe neutrality of mind. It is the Nazi propaganda which has maintained that a nation wanted to keep out of war as a neutral also is imposing upon itself neutrality in words and beliefs." The principle has since then often been confirmed in words and applied in practice — at times with some difficulties or exceptions.

25 This attitude is a principle related to the rejection of ideological neutrality — the right to criticize has become a duty to do so.

26 Sverker Aström, Sweden's Policy of Neutrality (Stockholm 1977), pp. 20.

27 Max Jacobson in Svenska Dagbladet, 9 October, 1983.

28 Modern Sweden has a strong tradition of upholding the rights of small States in international law and organizations.

29 For a catalogue of Swedish interests in disarmament negotiations cf. Nils Andrén/Nils Gyldén/Johan S. J. Lundin, Internationella rustningsbegränsningar och nationell säkerhet (International Arms Limitations and National Security), Stockholm 1979, pp. 12.

30 This point has been emphasized at least since 1960, when Undén warned against disarmament measures destabilizing the balance of power. Documents 1961, pp. 74—75.

31 Cf. Michael Howard (at the 1982 IISS Annual Conference), Adelphi Papers No. 184 (London 1983), pp. 17—26.

32 Cf. Bo K. A. Huldt, Swedish Disarmament Policy from the 1920s to the 1980s (Stockholm 1983) mimeo.

33 Ivor Jennings, Cabinet Government (Cambridge, England, 1937), p. 390.

34 Andrén, op. cit., p. 23.

35 See note 1.

36 Cf. Huldt, op. cit.

37 The Swedish nuclear issue has been reviewed by Gunnar Jervas, in: Sverige och kärnvapnen (Sweden and Nuclear Arms), Tempus (1981), pp. 40.

38 Bo Huldt/Erik Holm (eds.), Peace and Security after the Second World War (Stockholm 1945), p. 31.

39 Huldt, op. cit., H. Eek, Sveriges utrikespolitik och FN (Sweden's foreign policy and the United Nations), Skrifter utgivna av Utrikespolitiska institutet No. 9 (Stockholm 1955), p. 42.

40 Documents 1961, pp. 44—46; also Katarina Brodin, Undénplanen (The Undén Plan) (Stockholm 1966)

41 A Nordic non-nuclear zone is currently propagated by the Swedish Government. Cf. Johan Tunberger, Norden — en kärnvapenfri zon? (Northern Europe — a non-nuclear zone), (Stockholm 1982). Also S. Lodgaard/M. Thee, Nuclear Disengagement in Europe. Published for SIPRI and PUGWASH (London and New York 1983).

42 Documents 1959, pp. 22.

43 Especially from the Swedish chief disarmament negotiator, Alva Myrdal, whose bitterness is reflected in her book The Game of Disarmament (New York 1976).

44 The observatory (in Hagfors, county of Värmland) is operated by the National Defense Research Institute.

45 Cf. Andrén/Gyldén/Lundin, op. cit., passim, and studies by Johan S. J. Lundin, e. g. Considera-

tions in a Chemical Arms Control Treaty and the Concept of Amplified Verification, 7 FOA (Swedish Defense Research Institute), Reports (1973), pp. 1; Chemical Weapons: Too Late for Disarmament? 35 The Bulletin of Atomic Scientists (1979), pp. 10.

46 Dr. Rolf Björnerstedt, a physicist, and Mr. Jan Martenson, a diplomat.

47 Cf. note 41.

48 President Reagan in statement on START negotiations, 4 October, 1983.

49 TASS interview with Soviet Minister of Defense Ustinov, 30 July, 1983.

50 Cf. Huldt op. cit., and Jan Prawitz, Nedrustningsfragan och Svensk Säkerhetspolitik (The Disarmament Question and Swedish Security Policy), in: Internationella studier (Stockholm 1974) No. 4, and Ingemar Dörfer, Nordic Security Today: Sweden, in: Cooperation and Conflict (Oslo 1982) No. 4.

51 Cf. Huldt, op. cit., with references to Arnold Wolfers' distinction between milieu goals and possession goals in foreign policy, in: Discontent and Collaboration (Baltimore 1962).

52 Swedish diplomats have often given testimony to this effect...

53 President Reagan in a statement on START, 4 October, 1983.

54 TASS interview with Soviet Minister of Defense Ustinov, 30 July, 1983.

55 Huldt, op. cit., and Jan Prawitz, Nedrustningsfragan och Svensk Säkerhetspolitik (The Disarmament Question and Swedish Security Policy), Internationella studier (1974); Ingemar Dörfer, Nordic Security Today: Sweden, Cooperation and Conflict (1982), pp. 273.

56 Huldt, op. cit., with references to Arnold Wolfers' distinction between „milieu goals" and „possession goals" in foreign policy.

F. A. M. Alting von Geusau

J. F. Kennedy Institute, Center for International Studies, Tilburg

Between Lost Illusions and Apocalyptic Fears: Benelux Views on the European Neutrals

1. History

The Treaty of London in 1839 sealed the separation of The Netherlands and Belgium and the failure of British policy at the time of the Congress of Vienna to create a new State, large enough to function as a buffer against French expansion. The Netherlands—a small State ever since—decided on a foreign policy of aloofness from international complications and alliances with other States, at the time referred to as a 'hedgehog policy'. Aloofness, however, did not mean isolationism. The Netherlands remained active in trade and the international exchange of ideas. The two Peace Conferences of 1899 and 1907 took place in The Hague. Later, The Hague became the seat of the Peace Palace, which would host the Permanent Court of Justice since 1922 and the International Court of Justice after the Second World War. During the First World War, The Netherlands managed to remain a "neutral power". Belgium and Luxembourg (since 1867) were permanently neutralized under a guarantee of Great Britain, France, Prussia and Russia. Their neutrality was violated by Germany in 1914, and neutralization ceased to exist at the end of the war.

The three countries (Belgium as an original member, Luxembourg and The Netherlands through accession) joined the League of Nations and accepted, *inter alia,* the rules concerning sanctions in Art. 16 of the Covenant[1]. Upon the denunciation in 1936 of the Locarno Treaties by Hitler-Germany, Belgium and The Netherlands[2] unilaterally readopted a policy of neutrality and declared themselves to be no longer bound by the rules in Art. 16 of the Covenant. The three countries, nevertheless, were invaded and occupied by Germany. They joined the alliance of the United Nations against the Axis Powers (1942) and the United Nations in 1945. They gave up their policy of neutrality in the new circumstances of the post-war era. The three countries joined the 1948 Treaty of Brussels, the 1949 North Atlantic Treaty and the European Communities.

This brief historical review may already point to a difference in experience, likely to influence views on the present-day "European neutrals".

The Dutch policy of aloofness as it developed in the nineteenth century had its roots in Dutch political culture. It served the country well for a long period, both in terms of maintaining national independence and of playing a certain role in international relations. It was, expecially, morally satisfying. Traditions of such a nature nurture illusions that do not easily fade away.

Belgian neutrality, on the other hand, was the product of convenience for the then Great Powers. It disappeared in 1914, when Germany decided it was no longer convenient militarily to respect it. In the 1930s, Belgium, together with other small European States, hoped to avoid another occupation by declaring its neutrality. As a policy to assure national independence, neutrality in Belgium more definitely is seen, after May 1940, as a lost illusion.

2. A Comparison

The four European neutrals of today have a very different historical experience both from the Benelux countries and from each other:

a) Switzerland today still enjoys the same status of permanent neutrality, as Belgium did from 1839—1914. Although the guarantee of Swiss neutrality by the eight Great Powers of the Congresses of Vienna and in Paris 1815 has long ago lost its validity[3], the recognition of Swiss perpetual neutrality has become part of international law. In the two great wars of this century Switzerland has been able to maintain its neutrality. Since the Second World War, Switzerland has very strictly adhered to its interpretation of the status of neutrality, and has not (as yet) applied for admission to the United Nations.

b) Austria, as one of the successor States to the far from neutral Austro-Hungarian Empire, has no tradition of neutrality or "aloofness" comparable to either Switzerland or The Netherlands. Its permanent neutrality since 1955 as a status is best comparable—though in different political and strategic circumstances—to the status of Belgium after 1839. In case of major war, it stands no better chance to be respected than Belgian neutrality in 1914. Its interpretation of the status of neutrality is far less strict than that of Switzerland[4].

c) Sweden as a former major power, has no tradition of neutrality. During the two World Wars, it managed to remain a non-belligerent. After some hesitation in 1948 and the breakdown of alliance negotiations with Denmark and Norway in 1949, Sweden decided to continue alone a policy of armed non-involvement in the building up of the NATO and the Soviet alliance systems.

d) Finland, during the Second World War, had assured national survival by resisting both Soviet and German invasion. After the Second World War, the new balance of forces in Europe did not enable Finland to ignore Soviet opposition to closer relations with the Scandinavian countries. Finland—because of its successful wartime resistance against Soviet aggression—did manage, however, to escape the fate of Hungary, Czechoslovakia, Poland, Rumania and Bulgaria. Finland obtained a status of neutrality tolerated by the Soviet Union.

3. The Experiences of the Benelux Countries with Neutrality

From the vantage point of the Benelux countries, three of the four "European neutrals" are still to be considered as apprentices of neutrality. All three of them began their experiences after the Benelux countries had given up neutrality. The Benelux countries did so by necessity rather than by choice.

Before presenting Benelux views on the role of European neutrals, it may therefore be useful to offer Benelux experiences as neutral small powers.

Being neutral in Europe has been and still is to be distinguished in terms of a *status* in time of peace and in time of war and an *attitude or policy* in time of peace.

As a status or legal institution, neutrality belongs to the "laws of war". It has been defined[5] "as the attitude of impartiality adopted by third states towards belligerents and recognized by belligerents, such attitude creating rights and duties between the impartial states and the belligerents". It "cannot begin before the outbreak of war becomes known". Neutrality "ends with the cessation of war, or through a hitherto neutral state beginning war against one of the belligerents, or through one of the belligerents commencing war against a hitherto neutral state". Under special circumstances, the status of neutrality may be extended to periods of peace: The "perpetual" or "permanent" status of States which are neutralized by special treaties (Switzerland since 1815, Belgium from 1839 to 1914). Contrary to neutrality in time of war, the status of being neutralized lacks a definition of rights and duties. The neutralization of Switzerland and Belgium was an "advantage" extended to them by the Powers and involved the latters' guarantee of the integrity and inviolability of their territory. Austria's permanent neutrality was proclaimed by Austria to fulfill a Soviet condition for Austria's re-establishment as an independent State.

From the point of view of the neutralized State, such a status serves its interests if it is conducive to its neutrality in time of war. From the point of view of the guaranteeing powers, the status had been granted to serve their interests in maintaining a certain balance of power among themselves. In the case of Belgium (and Switzerland), neutralization was to serve the interest of containing France.

On the eve of the First World War, the balance of power and interests had become very different. Germany—as the strongest military power—had long ago made plans for violating Belgian neutrality for reasons of military convenience in case of a war with France.

The principal arguments for disregarding the legal commitment to respect Belgian neutrality were of a strategic nature: Through Belgium, German armies could bypass the French fortifications and win a quick victory over the French armies. In so doing, Great Britain might be prevented from joining the war on the French and Russian side; a war on two fronts might be avoided. A quick victory on the Western front would enable Germany to free its forces for the war on the Eastern front in time before the Russian armies had reached full strength through mobilization. Neither the British nor French reaffirmation of Belgian neutrality, nor Belgian adherence to its status proved helpful in keeping Belgium out of the war. The contrary may well have been true. The Germans, though, did gamble on the chance that Belgium would give in to their ultimatum (rather than defend itself) and Britain would not come to its rescue under the guarantee.

The *attitude or policy of neutrality in time of peace* is to be distinguished from the above-mentioned status. It is not based on a legal right or obligation. It is the outcome of a unilaterally declared and/or practiced policy of a State. As a policy, it always involves a refusal to conclude alliances with a major power. In the day-to-day conduct of foreign policy it may take the form of aloofness from and non-involvement with or a willingness to mediate and conciliate between adversaries.

In their first variant, such policies were conducted by The Netherlands (before 1914) and by both The Netherlands and Belgium prior to 1940.

In 1914, military considerations, rather than Dutch policy, kept The Netherlands out of the war. The sweep through Southern Limburg (included in the Schlieffen Plan) was given up in the amended plan of attack (by von Moltke).

In 1940, Dutch and Belgian neutrality, together with the military weakness of these countries, made them an easy target for German invasion. With a state of war already in existence among Germany, Great Britain and France, their neutrality had lost its meaning. German forces invaded Belgium, Luxembourg and The Netherlands without any previous ultimatum. All that neutrality had provided them with was unwillingness to take defensive measures in concert with their (future) allies and unpreparedness to confront invasion and occupation.

The lessons which the Benelux countries have learned so far in the course of this century are threefold:

1. Neither the status of guaranteed neutralization, nor their policy of neutrality could keep them out of war or secure their territorial integrity.
2. Military considerations on the part of the strongest European power were decisive for the violation (or non-violation) of their territorial integrity.
3. Neutrality made them less defensible and less prepared to face invasion and occupation.

Most Benelux observers will probably concur with the opinion that military considerations *only* kept Switzerland out of the two World Wars.

4. Post-War Benelux Views

In the early months of the Second World War, the then neutral States—in Europe and elsewhere—together with the United States, considered the possibility of joining together for the purpose of laying the foundations for a peaceful post-war world order. When Hitler's armies overran Western Europe in 1940, US policies began to change towards support for Great Britain—formalized in the Atlantic Charter of August 1941.

The German attack on the USSR, the Japanese attack on Pearl Harbor, and the German declaration of war on the United States put an end to these efforts. On 1 January 1942, twenty-six nations concluded a wartime coalition against the Axis Powers, known as the "Declaration by United Nations". Twenty-one nations adhered to it before the end of the war. Among them were all former neutrals with the exception of Sweden, Switzerland, Finland, and Denmark. All of them (with the exception of Switzerland) became members of the United Nations[6]. It was clearly understood that the status of neutrality was incompatible with membership in the Organization. At the end of the Second World War, neutrality as a legal institution had virtually ceased to exist.

Soon thereafter, with the onset of the "Cold War" in Europe and the painful East-West division of the European subcontinent, the problem of neutrality re-emerged, but in a very different form.

On the one hand, the division of Europe into two "hostile camps"—as proclaimed by the 1947 Cominform Declaration—made neutrality ideologically inconceivable as a policy. The democratic States of Europe appeared to have only a choice between forming an alliance among themselves and with the United States or submission to Soviet political influence or Soviet totalitarian repression. As we saw already, the Benelux countries opted for the first alternative. In their opinion, the division of Europe excluded a policy of neutrality as an acceptable choice for any other European State. They had little or no understanding for the policies of Sweden and Switzerland. They understood the fate of Finland, but feared a similar fate for themselves in the absence of a clear policy in favor of alliance and integration[7].

On the other hand, the East-West conflict reduced the United Nations to impotence as an institution to maintain international peace and security in any conflict involving the major Powers. A status of neutrality had been considered incompatible with Art. 2 para. 5 and Chapter VII of the Charter in particular. In the aftermath of the 1950 Korean conflict, however, it became increasingly clear that enforcement action by the Security Council no longer was among the tasks the Council could perform. If the United Nations were still called upon to deal with peace and security, it was merely as a framework for mediation and disarmament negotiations. In the mid-fifties, neutrality thus re-emerged in two new forms: the policy of non-alignment originally promoted by Yugoslavia, India and Egypt; and the status of being neutralized, accepted by Austria.

The East-West compromise on Austria in 1955 was a product of the first (brief) period of East-West *détente.*

The movement of non-alignment reflected both the new influence of the "Third World" and the stalemate in East-West relations. Yugoslavia's prominent role in the movement can be explained by its special position as a "socialist" country no longer belonging to the Soviet system. Yugoslavia opted for non-alignment as a policy to maintain its independence from the Soviet Union. The first period of East-West *détente* thus strengthened the case for neutrality in Europe, whereas non-alignment activated the policies of some of the European neutrals. Both developments restored the respectability of neutrality (especially) in the eyes of the smaller member States of NATO.

The respectability of a policy of neutrality in the eyes of smaller European States has since then been further enhanced by four international political developments:

1. the growing influence of the "Third World", non-aligned States and their emphasis on economic development, as the major world problem (next to, or instead of the East-West conflict);
2. the growing problem of nuclear weapons (proliferation, the "balance of terror" and the ongoing arms build-up);
3. the coming, since 1962, of East-West and especially Soviet-American *détente;*
4. the search for a West European identity and world role, distinct from the United States; promoted originally by French President Charles de Gaulle and "Europeanized" since 1969 as a result of the new German *Ostpolitik* and changes in British foreign policy.

The evaluations of these developments were different among the member States of NATO and of the European Communities. They were dealt with, moreover, in a variety of international organizations and conferences, in which the search for common Western positions was no longer deemed to be feasible or attractive. Like other smaller States, the Benelux countries—The Netherlands in particular—sought to enhance their role in multilateral organizations by operating more independently from their allies and by working in concert with more like-minded States on the issues under consideration.

The respectability of (some of) the European neutrals was thus further strengthened by the possibility of developing common positions between allied and neutral smaller States on a variety of international issues.

During the late 1960s and the decade of the 1970s, the cohesion of the Atlantic Alliance has, moreover, been severely undermined by the American involvement in the Vietnam conflict, the increasingly uneasy relations between the United States and the European Communities and increasing divergencies in the policies of *détente* pursued by the allies separately. In Western Europe, a profound change in the intellectual and political climate has taken place. In the minds of many West Europeans, the image of the USA as the democratic ally to be relied upon changed to one of an unreliable, if not dangerous, superpower. At the same time, the image of the Soviet Union as the totalitarian threat to peace improved to one of a threatened superpower. The fundamental difference between democratic government and totalitarian rule thus tends to be concealed by such confusing abstract notions as "military blocs", "deterrence systems" or superpowers. The similarity thus evoked between the Western and Soviet alliance systems has among its consequences in the West the view that a policy of neutrality is no longer ideologically inconceivable.

For many in the Benelux countries, a policy of neutrality thus tends to become attractive rather than only respectable. Such is the case in particular in The Netherlands for yet two other reasons: (1) the unfavorable change in the East-West military balance; and (2) the necessity for the North Atlantic Alliance to redress the imbalance by modernization programs. The first trend has increased the fear of Soviet power and the willingness to compromise; the second has increased fear of nuclear war and a preference for arms-control-only policies. Since the early 1970s, various Dutch governments have advocated a reduction of the role of nuclear weapons as a primary objective. A tendency can be observed to be more concerned about NATO modernization programs than about the reason for such programs: the massive and continuing build-up of Soviet military power.

Benelux views on the European neutrals thus have evolved from minimal comprehension to increasing attraction. They are attracted—positively—by the neutrals' policies of mediation between East and West, and—negatively—by their advantage of non-involvement in the painful allied decisions to maintain adequate military strength and political solidarity.

On the level of the Benelux governments, a return to a policy of neutrality—i.e. withdrawal from NATO—is not under consideration. The neutrality of Finland, Sweden, Austria and Switzerland ist accepted as a political fact if not an all-European interest in the present world situation. On specific issues—for example in the field of arms control—cooperation is sought especially with Sweden and Austria.

On the level of political parties and public opinion, the situation is more complex. The issue is not alignment versus neutrality, nor is there any major interest in the role played by the European neutrals as such. The underlying problems in Belgium and The Netherlands are the break-down of domestic political consensus on basic external security policies, and a threefold loss of political confidence: between government and people, among European governments, and between Western Europe and North America. On the left side of the political spectrum, fear of nuclear war, anti-American feelings and ideological affinity with the Communist parties produce what is referred to as neutralist tendencies. These tendencies, however, are closer to appeasement than to policies of neutrality. On the right side of the political spectrum, emphasis is placed on the continuing Soviet threat. A minority[8] might favor a strong Europe more independent from the United States (from fear of isolationist tendencies in the US). The majority favors the maintenance of NATO. The political center is divided. It combines a clear and continuing commitment to NATO with strong emphasis on arms control and reduction policies. It is this emphasis which brings them closer to the views of some of the European neutrals than either left- or right-of-center politicians.

5. Evaluating the Role of the European Neutrals

The role a country plays in inter-State relations ultimately depends on its capacity to defend itself if attacked. This capacity itself depends on its internal strength, geography, political-strategic position, and the most likely threats it faces. As was the case for the Benelux countries in 1914 and 1940, the European neutrals are threatened primarily by the strongest military power in Europe, which today is the USSR. Individually, they are unable to resist this threat. All they can hope to achieve by their foreign policies and defense preparations is to convince the Kremlin that it is more advantageous from a military point of view to bypass their territories in case of war. Measured by this yardstick, their role must be considered as very limited and comparable to the earlier Dutch role; Geneva, Vienna and Helsinki are for East-West meetings what The Hague had been for the 1899 and 1907 Peace Conferences.

The present East-West no-peace and no-war relationship, however, is also different from the pre-World War I relationship.

The post-war alliances are open and multilateral arrangements for self-defense and have grown into permanent organizational frameworks for policy coordination and integrated military structures.

Western and neutral States in Europe alike are confronted with Soviet "total foreign policy", or totalitarian diplomatic warfare, aimed at preserving Soviet hegemony in Eastern Europe and at achieving the strategic defeat of the West without having to fight a war.

The Western allied and neutral States share a basic interest in avoiding that Soviet power and control further expand over Europe. They equally share the opinion that the violation of human rights anywhere must be the concern of all States in East and West. They also share interests in improving economic relations and a free flow of persons, information and ideas throughout Europe. Western and neutral States, by the very nature of their political systems, are unable to conduct a total foreign policy.

This essentially asymmetrical relationship between East and West—in policy aims, methods of operation and the nature of the political regimes—leaves no room for a convergence of policies or reconciliation. Active mediation by the European neutrals as a consequence is a role without an attainable purpose, beyond that of providing assistance to gain time in efforts to prevent war. *Détente* in this relationship, unfortunately, has been little more than a common denominator for fundamentally different policies.

Attention to the role of the European neutrals in the search for peace and security is related primarily to CSCE. In fact, it was CSCE which established the European neutrals as an identifiable group, with Austria, Sweden and Switzerland as its nucleus.

In the Benelux countries, the role of the European neutrals began to receive attention especially during the second phase of CSCE.

Benelux interest in the role of the European neutrals concerned two aspects. First, the European neutrals played a role in reaching compromises on specific texts or package deals. Second, the activities of the European neutrals promoted a sense of common interest among the smaller Powers (whether neutral or Western, and sometimes including Romania) as distinct from the major powers. This common position included such military aspects as confidence-building measures. Such a joint role has been made possible by the specific characteristics of CSCE as a multilateral conference operating on the principle of consensus and aiming no further than at a political and legally non-binding document. It does not extend beyond CSCE or to other East-West arms control negotiations. After the Helsinki "Summit Conference" and two Follow-up Conferences, one must unfortunately conclude that the role of the European neutrals and of the wider circle of smaller States has become very limited indeed even within CSCE.

CSCE itself has not contributed to reducing East-West tension; it may even have sharpened the division of our continent. In this situation, the European neutrals have little more to offer than Geneva, Vienna or Helsinki as suitable places to keep East-West negotiations going.

Limited as this definition of the role of the European neutrals may sound, it is not without significance. In the East-West no-peace-no-war situation, the continuation of negotiations remains important in the efforts to prevent the outbreak of war.

Notes

1 Art. 16: 1. Should any Member of the League resort to war in disregard of its covenants under Articles 12, 13 or 15, it shall *ipso facto* be deemed to have committed an act of war against all other Members of the League, which hereby undertake immediately to subject it to the severance of all trade or financial relations, the prohibition of all intercourse between their nationals and the nationals of the covenant-breaking State, and the prevention of all financial, commercial or personal intercourse between the nationals of the covenant-breaking State and the nationals of any other State, whether a Member of the League or not.
2. It shall be the duty of the Council in such case to recommend to the several Governments concerned what effective military, naval or air force the Members of the League shall severally contribute to the armed forces to be used to protect the covenants of the League.
3. The Members of the League agree, further, that they will mutually support one another in the financial and economic measures which are taken under this Article, in order to minimize the loss and inconvenience resulting from the above measures, and that they will mutually support one another in resisting any special measures aimed at one of their number by the covenant-breaking State, and that they will take the necessary steps to afford passage through their territory to the forces of any of the Members of the League which are co-operating to protect the covenants of the League.
4. Any Member of the League which has violated any covenant of the League may be declared to be no longer a Member of the League by a vote of the Council concurred in by the Representatives of all the other Members of the League represented thereon.

2 With Denmark, Finland, Norway, Spain and Sweden.

3 The eight Powers were: Austria, France, Great Britain, Portugal, Prussia, Russia, Spain and Sweden/Norway.

4 E.g. the statement by Chancellor Julius Raab to the National Council on 23 March 1960 during the debate on Austrian participation in EFTA, 2 Österreichische Zeitschrift für Außenpolitik (1961), pp. 186.

5 L. Oppenheim/H. Lauterpacht, International Law (Vol. II: Disputes, War and Neutrality, 7th ed., London 1963), p. 653, 666, 671.

6 Sweden in 1946, Finland in 1955. All others were original members.

7 Hence the term "Finlandization", which expresses a fear rather than a judgment of Finnish foreign policy.

8 In the Benelux countries this minority is much smaller than in France or even in the Federal Republic of Germany.

Arne Olav Brundtland

Norwegian Institute of International Affairs, Oslo

The Value of the Swedish and the Finnish Policies of Neutrality to the Security of Norway

1. Introduction

The value for Norway of the Swedish and Finnish policies of neutrality can hardly be exaggerated. Swedish and Finnish neutrality form a fundamental part of the international preconditions for the Norwegian approach to security policy. The defense of Norway in the present situation cannot seriously be contemplated without consideration of these external conditions. On the other hand, Norwegian security policy is of particular importance to the security of both Sweden and Finland. But this latter aspect is by definition beyond the topic of this paper to be presented at the Laxenburg conference on the value of neutrality in present-day security policies in Europe.

A prerequisite for the pattern of security in Northern Europe—often referred to as the "Nordic Balance"[1]—is the sovereign right of all Nordic States to formulate national security policies without the interference of any other Northern European State. There exists, therefore, a basis for mutual respect and understanding of the individual security policies pursued by each of the Nordic States.

No Nordic State sees its problem of security as emanating from any Nordic source. The general security problem of the Nordic States stems from the potential for conflict between non-Nordic States into which the Nordic States might be drawn. And because of differences in geographical position, historical experiences and defensive capabilities, the individual Nordic States have embarked upon their own distinctive security policies in order to cope with this international problem.

2. Nordic Security Policy

The different security policies of the individual Nordic States could briefly be summed up in the following points; the contours of these policies were laid down under the impact of the emergence of the "Cold War" in Europe in the years 1947—1949, and their essence has remained unchanged up to now.

a) Finland pursues a policy of neutrality on the basis of the Treaty of Friendship, Cooperation and Mutual Assistance concluded with the Soviet Union in 1948. The treaty is designed around a specific scenario based on a possible German attack, or aggression on the part of States allied with Germany, on Finland, or on the Soviet Union but using Finnish territory as a transit corridor. In the event of such an attack, Finland has pledged herself in accordance with her rights and obligations as a sovereign country to resist the attack with all the means at her disposal. If necessary, Finland will either receive aid from the Soviet Union to repel such an attack, or the two countries might cooperate militarily in repelling the aggressor. The rendering of Soviet assistance is subject to a separate agreement in each concrete case. In the event of a threat of an attack as envisaged in the treaty, the two parties are to consult about how to meet, not the threat, but the actual attack.
   Under the Peace Treaty of 1947, Finnish military forces have been limited to a number not exceeding 42,000 troops, and must not possess certain types of weapons. But Finland has not been prevented from maintaining general conscription and has, for the time being, an ability to field about 700.000 reservists. Nevertheless, Finland is considered to have a somewhat weak military apparatus, particularly with regard to weapons and other equipment[2].
b) Sweden pursues a policy under the well-established formula of „freedom from alliances in peace-time in order to stay neutral in war". Swedish defense is considered to be rather substantial, although it is all conventional since Sweden has renounced the option of producing nuclear weapons.
   Both Sweden and Finland thus pursue policies of neutrality. But the special circumstances of their respective policies make it mandatory to undertake a separate evaluation of their respective neutrality. No country has the exclusive right to determine the particular content of the policy of neutrality abstractly. There might be as many types of neutrality as there are countries which attempt to pursue neutrality[3].
c) Norway and Denmark fall into another category since they both have chosen to be members of a Great Power alliance, namely NATO. But both countries have decided to pursue a policy of not allowing the basing of foreign troops in times of peace, nor the storage of nuclear weapons, on their territories. Denmark maintains a particular national defense profile with regard to the Danish island of Bornholm in the Baltic. Norway maintains a low military profile in the North, both with regard to allied participation in military manoeuvres and with regard to national defensive measures in forward positions, that is, with regard to the country of Finnmark which borders both the Soviet Union and Finland. Norway concentrates her national defense effort in the county of

Troms, which borders Finland as well as Sweden, but which is about 400 kilometres (by air) away from the Soviet border.

A most important feature of the security policies of the Nordic countries is their high degree of stability and predictability.

All of these countries seem eager to stick to the policy lines they once selected. None of them is likely to alter its policy because of minor provocations. These policies are meant to hold both in periods of international *détente,* as well as in periods of high international tensions. They have stood the test of fluctuations in the international situation during a period of more than 35 years.

3. The Military Relevance of Swedish and Finnish Neutrality and Security Policies for Norway

But this having been said, all countries naturally keep the international situation under constant observation in order to be sure that their policies continue to provide adequate security. In Norway, in particular, the security debate is conducted with regard to the measures to be undertaken in order to maintain the proper balance between deterrence and reassurance so as to avoid both provocation and subjugation. Norwegian security policy is of an intrinsically political nature.

The security policies of Finland and Sweden are thus "givens" for Norwegian security planners. One does not try to stimulate any alteration of the security policies of the neighboring States. But one does try to follow developments there in order to check whether one's own policy really confers adequate protection. And it should be kept in mind that even though Finnish and Swedish security policies are of great importance to Norway, the real challenge to Norwegian security is posed by the Soviet Union. The response to this challenge is based upon a continuous evaluation of measures to be taken either by national means or in cooperation with the other partners of NATO. At present a particular problem is presented by the huge build-up of the Soviet navy and the general improvement in the ability of the Soviet Union to launch strong military attacks over substantial distances. The answer for diminishing the probability and the possibility of a Soviet attack is at present primarily sought by a policy of prepositioning allied military equipment on Norwegian soil. The most controversial of these policies is naturally connected with the prepositioning of equipment and weapons for a US Amphibious Brigade in mid-Norway, and for prepositioning equipment at Norwegian airfields for US military aircraft, the so-called COB program.

Norway does this in order to maintain her non-basing policy which alternatively would have been nullified by a call for allied reinforcements either in peace-time or early in a crisis situation. The policy of prepositioning of material is a policy that allows Norwegian decision-makers more flexibility and more time. A possible renunciation of the policy of prepositioning could convey the impression that Norway would find herself isolated behind forward Soviet naval positions in the event of a show-down.

Thus, the Norwegian evaluation of the security positions of Finland and Sweden, even if these are of great importance, is not the only, nor probably the most important factor in current Norwegian security calculations.

Let us then examine the roles of Finland and Sweden, respectively, with regard to Norwegian security.

The value of the two countries as a military buffer should be appreciated against the background of the recognition of the North Norwegian coastline and the exits of the Baltic, including the Southern tip of Norway, as the two most important sub-regions in a calculation of military strategy.

A war in Northern Europe might first and foremost take place as a race with regard to these two sub-regions, either with the aim of denying them to the opponent, or with regard to their possible use by the party who could take possession of them first.

In the North, Norway, as already indicated, has concentrated its forces in the county of Troms. In the South, Norwegian defense planning takes account of the combined Danish and German capabilities to provide warning time in the event of war by preventing Warsaw Pact forces from using the Baltic exits. The military defense of Southern Norway is closely related to Norway's ability to mobilize her army and her coastal artillery. The necessary warning time is of importance.

A strong Swedish defense necessary to prevent the use of Southern Sweden for military transit plays an important role in this regard. This might be illuminated by reflecting on the alternative, namely that a Warsaw Pact attack could be channelled through Sweden. That would make the defense of Norway much more complicated, and one might, under such conditions, really reconsider the policy of not having standing forces in Southern Norway in peace-time.

In the North, the Swedish defense of Northern Sweden plays a similar role. An attack on Northern Norway might come either from the seaside or across the Soviet border, possibly also through Finnish territory. The Norwegian defense effort is complicated as it is. But if an attacker could, in addition, use Northern Sweden for transit, the whole concept of Norwegian concentration in Troms county would have to be re-examined. The use of Swedish territory in the North might lead to isolation of the Northern Norwegian defense forces and thereby seriously complicate Norwegian and Allied plans for reinforcing the Northern forces in time of hostilities.

The value of Northern Finland as a buffer is also considerable, although it periodically becomes the object of public scrutiny and criticism.

Neither Norwegian authorities nor Allied authorities disregard the value of the vast area of Northern Finland. But from time to time one does discuss the real ability of the Finnish military to check the use of Northern Finland by Soviet forces and the will of the Finns to do so under different circumstances.

General Rogers, Supreme Commander of the Allied Forces Europe, in January 1983 made critical remarks about the Finnish ability and will to protect Northern Finland against Soviet military use. But after further examination of the question, the General in February publicly acknowledged that his appreciation of the problem had been too pessimistic. Norwegian military personalities, such as the commander of the Troms Territorial Defense, Colonel Lerheim, have also made critical remarks in the same vein. But his evaluation has not been supported by leading national defense officials. On the contrary, he was publicly rebuked for his statements by the chief of the Norwegian Army, General Eios, in June 1983.

An appreciation of the military contingencies connected with Northern Finland should be made bearing in mind a number of factors. Among these are the fact that there are good roads in the East-West direction in the area, but also that these roads run over big bridges that could be demolished in a crisis situation. The territory is vast and easy to observe. No enemy could travel in the area without being sighted at an early stage.

The Finnish defense forces in Northern Finland, both army and airforce, have been steadily improved, and Finland is set on a policy to continue this build-up.

President Koivisto said to the Helsinki daily newspaper „Helsingin Sanomat" in June 1983 that this policy would be maintained. And he even added that it would be pleasing to Finland if the Finnish build-up could help neighbouring States to moderate their build-up in their respective territories adjacent to Northern Finland.

We might conclude that even considering that Finnish Lapland is more exposed in an East-West military conflict than Swedish Lapland, Finnish Lapland has an intrinsic buffer value to Norwegian defense.

In more general terms, the whole of Finland and the whole of Sweden function as military buffers for Norway. Southern Finland might, however, be of less value to Norway as a buffer than Northern Finland, even though the defensive efforts for Southern Finland are considerable. The over-all defense of Sweden, on the other hand, is of paramount importance to Norwegian defense planning.

We have commented upon the fact that the defense of the Southern part of Sweden and the Northern part of Sweden provides buffer services for Norwegian defense in the South and in the North. But the very fact that Sweden as a whole is well defended, in particular with a strong and modern airforce, eases the defense of Norway in a number of ways. This can be understood if one takes into account that the Norwegian border with Sweden has almost no Norwegian defense. In addition, there are almost no standing army units in Norway South of Troms county, if one disregards the Royal Guard and military training centers. If Norwegian defense planning was unable to count on a strong Swedish defense, the over-all Norwegian defense problem would be of a totally different nature.

This problem could be contemplated against the background of various alternative Swedish defense postures. The weaker the Swedish buffer, the more unmanageable would be the Norwegian defense situation.

Norway would either have to spend disproportionally more on national defense, or would in the event of strongly weakened Swedish defense, have to contemplate the permanent alteration of her non-basing policy by stationing Allied forces on Norwegian territory on a permanent basis.

4. The Relevance of Swedish and Finnish Peace-Time Security Policies for Norway

This leads us to the realm of peace-time security policy. The value of stable Swedish and Finnish security policies for Norway has already been stated in this paper. The problem of evaluating the effects of possible changes of these policy lines on Norwegian security policy is of a different category, since the basic components of the Swedish, Finnish and Norwegian security policies differ in their nature.

Let us start with Finland. The nature of Finnish security policy is probably best understood by reference to the basic dictum that for Finnish security foreign policy is of paramount importance. Finnish security policy is managed on the political level in the sense that one tries to keep military factors away from current calculations. One often hears that it is only when this policy has failed that the military will enter the scene. Under normal conditions, one tries to keep the military invisible. The function of the military is thus to render support to the policy of neutrality. But its profile must not be so high that the policy of friendly relations with the Soviet Union could be misinterpreted. Finnish military manoeuvres are conducted on a territorial basis in a *"tous azimuts"* fashion without any identification of a possible enemy.

The Norwegian tradition is different. Norwegian forces play the role of making the security policy of deterrence credible. Norwegian forces stage both national manoeuvres and manoeuvres with contingents from other Allied countries. The military profile in Norwegian security policy is higher than the corresponding Finnish profile.

Both Norwegian and Finnish security policies try to help keep tensions with the Soviet Union at the lowest possible level. One can probably say that Finland, in this respect, is more successful than Norway, but the different positions of the two countries also place them in different relations with the Soviet Union.

Finland would try much more eagerly, and with much more success, to avoid tension by accommodating the Soviet Union in accordance with the "Paasikivi-Kekkonen line" of neutrality and friendly relations, thereby risking a higher degree of dependence on Soviet goodwill. Finland is a master in the art of not saying "no" to the Soviet Union but helping the Soviet Union to say "yes" to Finland.

The Norwegian tradition is different. In times of tension, Norway is more prone to demonstrate her military capabilities and the capabilities of her allies. She is more disposed to say "no" to the Soviet Union at the risk of a less cooperative Soviet Union, but with the bonus of a feeling of a more solid security based on deterrence. Nevertheless, the relations of the Soviet Union with "capitalist" Finland and Norway, are among the least complicated of the relations the Soviet Union enjoys, even if those with her neighbours of various "socialist" persuasions are included.

A prime interest in Finnish security policy is to maintain the most cordial relations possible with the Soviet Union. This was successfully achieved in the immediate post-war years under the able leadership of President Paasikivi. He conducted a policy of caution. As an example, he managed to keep Finland neutral and to strengthen Finland's neutral image even though refraining from claiming neutrality or even without using the word neutrality in public speeches.

The continuation of the Paasikivi line by President Kekkonen (1956—1982) added a more dynamic aspect to Finnish security policy. Kekkonen embarked on a policy of winning recognition of Finnish neutrality both in the East and in the West, thereby providing a broader basis for this policy. The more successful he was in obtaining Western recognition of Finnish neutrality, the more convinced the Soviet Union could be that Finland would not conspire with anti-Soviet regimes in the West. And the surer the Soviet leaders could be that Finland would be faithful to the policy of neutrality, the more trustful the relations between the two countries could be. Kekkonen thereby managed to broaden the basis of support for the Finnish policy of neutrality.

But there is also another line in Kekkonen's policy which could be termed a predisposition for examining the secondary threat in order to influence the primary threat. Here I might add that the concept of a primary threat and a secondary threat is foreign to Finnish official declarations. It is an invention of observers in the West.

This line in Kekkonen's policy rested on the logic that the most important consideration of the Soviet leadership would be to keep their main opponents on the international scene as far away from Finland as possible. In this connection, the Swedish policy of neutrality was a great help since it, too, helped keep American, German or NATO influence in general at a distance. With regard to Denmark and Norway, but in particular Norway, the Finnish security interests were, of course, served by the low profile of Norwegian NATO membership (non-basing, non-storage, restrictions in the North). But, according to Kekkonen's way of thinking, it could be further served by additional guarantees that these policies would not be undermined by further Norwegian integration into NATO's general policies and thus the subordination to the leadership of the bigger powers in NATO. Or, it might be served by Norway's acceptance of an even lower security policy profile.

In line with such thinking, Mr. Kekkonen, at the time when he was Prime Minister, indicated that it would serve Finnish security if Norway and Denmark, like Sweden, embarked on a policy of neutrality. Later on, in the 1960s, he presented two ideas which continue to be upheld by Finnish foreign policy. One was his idea that the Nordic States should form a nuclear weapon-free zone by treaty; this became known as the so-called Kekkonen Plan.

The other was his idea that Norway and Finland should make arrangements that could further stabilize the peace of the Norwegian-Finnish border in the North: the "border pact" idea.

Both these ideas could help make the unilateral Norwegian restraints more resistent to change by linking them (and thereby modifying them) to multilateral arrangements to which non-NATO States would also be parties.

These two ideas were for many years considered to be "non-starters" because of Norwegian and Danish opposition. The Nordic NATO States, Norway and Denmark, observed, on the one hand, that the North of Europe, in reality, already was nuclear weapon-free and that an agreement would not alter this situation. A debate could, on the contrary, lead to unfounded speculations. On the other hand, the two States were reluctant to have their hands tied in the event that they might desire to exercise the option of calling in Allied nuclear weapons, perhaps in a crisis situation.

One has observed that the possibility of a change in the Norwegian policy of restraint was hinted at in connection with the Soviet-Finnish "note crisis" of 1961. At that time, it was thought to have strengthened President Kekkonen's hand in his conversations with Premier Nikita Khrushchev. But the risk of further possible use by Norwegian and Danish authorities of the option—even if this seems very unlikely—could entail complications for Finland[4].

The idea of a nuclear weapon-free Northern Europe has, however, been given a new lease of life by its sudden acceptance in Norwegian politics during the winter and spring of 1980/81. The idea of such a zone—preferably seen in a wider European context—is no longer rejected, but the models for this zone differ among the Norwegian political parties.

A main problem with the zone idea is that it seems impossible to combine the renunciation of the use of nuclear weapons in war, on the one hand, and the principal doctrine of NATO, flexible response, on the other. The latter is based on the notion that one should not reject the right and possiblility of opting for a first use of nuclear weapons in the event of otherwise losing the conventional battle.

One could probably say that the effect of the Kekkonen Plan has been considerable due to its frequent renewal over the years. But one could perhaps also add that, under present conditions, any further pressure, be it from Finland or from Sweden, which under Premier Olof Palme is supporting the idea, could be counterproductive with respect to the Norwegian and Danish governments, if not to important minorities in their parliaments[5].

Nor is the idea of a border pact dead with the Finnish presidential succession from Kekkonen to Koivisto. President Koivisto seems to be just as eager as Kekkonen to push the idea. But he has apparently selected another strategy. He is now indicating an examination of the idea step by step. One might start with parallel public declarations instead of going for a mutual pact. The parallel declaration approach is perhaps more effective, since it is less far-reaching. But it nevertheless affects security and Allied military cooperation in an area which is of paramount importance to Norwegian security. The present Norwegian conservative government appears to lack any disposition to follow Koivisto's idea[6].

Apart from Prime Minister Olof Palme's three approaches to the nuclear weapons problem, which will be discussed below, current Swedish security policies center around the submarine violations of Swedish territorial waters and the related problem of maintaining the relatively high level of Swedish defense spending.

These constitute separate problem areas. On the nuclear level, the Nordic zone has already been mentioned. There are naturally different models to be considered also as seen from the point of view of Swedish interests. One particular problem is the possibility of the inclusion of the Baltic Sea, either in part, or as a whole. Another are the different ideas as to what kind of Soviet concessions should be demanded. There is also the problem of how to start and structure negotiations. A prime Swedish concern has been to avoid models of the nuclear-free zone which could limit Swedish sovereignty in security matters. "The policy of neutrality is something which we determine ourselves", is a famous Swedish dictum. Yet, freedom of action for political manoeuvres might be smaller than one first might imagine.

The idea put forth by the Palme Commission of a corridor free from certain battlefield nuclear weapons along the intra-German border is another point of controversy. But this does not so directly impinge upon Nordic security policy. The same could be said about the resolution sponsored by Sweden and Mexico on the freezing of nuclear weapons which was adopted by the UN General Assembly in 1982.

But both ideas are widely discussed by the Norwegian public and they are factors for the re-examination of nuclear policies which might further stimulate the broad parliamentary idea of the need for a re-examination of the flexible response doctrine.

All this interest in nuclear weapons problems naturally helps to cement the idea that Norway neither in the present nor in the future should consider any nuclear option. A change here, and probably it has already taken place, would alter the Nordic security situation in a way which might be difficult to comprehend, since the existence of a Danish and Norwegian nuclear option has been part and parcel of the Nordic Balance.

The general problem of Swedish defense spending could have implications for Norwegian security, much in line with what has been mentioned in previous paragraphs about military scenarios. Even with some reductions of her armed forces, Sweden would, and this is the Norwegian over-all appreciation, continue to be a relatively strong nation in conventional armament. The strength, preparedness and actual deployment of the Swedish defense forces are of considerable importance to Norway.

The submarine incidents could be examined from different angles. The main difficulty is perhaps that there is no consensus as to the interpretation of the events. One does not know whether Sweden in reality is about to enter a new security situation. Declarations by high Swedish officials, such as Prime Minister Palme in the Stockholm daily "Dagens Nyheter" of 7 October 1983, have been stressing that the Swedish security line remains steady, although he, too, says he is mystified by the submarine incidents.

Relations between Sweden and the Soviet Union have been moving towards a stage of higher tension as a result of these incidents. It is difficult to judge what the future impact of this trend will be.

It seems to me that Norway has a stake of her own in this connection. It would be in the interest of Norwegian security that Sweden improve her ability to handle submarine incidents in order to maintain respect for her territorial integrity and neutrality.

If Sweden has to diminish her over-all defense in order to be better equipped to handle submarine incidents, it might be in the interest of Norway that the lessening of preparedness should not be projected to the flanks, that is to say to Swedish Lapland and the South of Sweden. Norway is better served by a relative weakening of the defense of central Sweden. But this might not coincide with the thinking in Stockholm. The Swedish flanks are more important to Norway than the central area of Sweden because international conflicts, which most certainly will involve Norway before they reach Sweden, might involve Sweden's flanks before they affect the core region.

Generally speaking, the way both Finland and Sweden have defined their security line is of considerable value to Norway as well. Changes in their security line and military preparedness may be felt in Norway, too. A lowering of their defenses and a weakening of their policies of neutrality as compared to present-day lines could be perceived as a negative factor in Norwegian security. For the two countries the maintenance of the status quo seems to be the best solution to their security problems.

In this paper we have so far dealt with the three different States, Norway, Sweden and Finland, disregarding the domestic debate that takes place also in the field of national security in all three of them. Basically, one might state that changes of government in any of these States in the post-war period have had little impact on the respective national security policies.

By and large, this might still be the case today. But all Nordic countries, like most other democratic countries, these days experience a keener public interest in security problems, in particular with regard to nuclear weapons.

The democratic debate on security could alter national priorities "from within". Whether this would be of significance as compared with the challenges to national security stemming from the international system, is hard to judge. But a wider democratization of security policies certainly produces new problems for the diplomatic efforts to curb the arms race.

For a variety of reasons, there is a freer national security debate both in the two neutral nations under consideration, Sweden and Finland, and in Norway.

A freer democratic discussion makes it more difficult to observe the well-established rule of non-interference by any Nordic State in the security affairs of any other.

5. Postscript

With regard to Norway, the domestic debate on security, which has been rather heated in 1982 and 1983, particularly because of disagreement over the strategy for achieving the objectives of the "dual track decision" of NATO, calmed down during the spring of 1984. The Foreign Relations Committee of the *Storting* (Parliament) agreed on a broad national platform with regard to security issues in May, and the *Storting* further demonstrated the new consensus subsequently.

Since the new consensus reopens questions like nuclear-free zones (provided they are part of a broader international framework), there exist new possibilities for joint efforts in Northern Europe.

Notes

1 For a short discussion of the Nordic Balance see Arne Olav Brundtland, The Nordic Balance and its possible Relevance for Europe, in: Daniel Frei (ed.), Sicherheit durch Gleichgewicht? (Zurich 1982), pp. 119 ff.

2 There is an increase in the literature on Finnish security policy by a variety of observers and experts involved. For an introduction see Max Jacobson, Finnish Neutrality: A Study of Finnish Foreign Policy Since the Second World War (London 1968).

3 There is no comprehensive work in English on either Norwegian or Swedish post-World War II security policy, whereas there exists a great number of books and articles, mostly in Norwegian and Swedish respectively. Cooperation and Conflict, the Nordic Journal on International Affairs, published by the Nordic Cooperation Committee for International Politics, may be particularly useful to anybody interested in further details.

4 See note 1.

5 It should however be added that the new consensus, mentioned in the postscript below, might provide a basis for easier communication across national borders on this matters.

6 Kaare Willoch's conservative minority government was formed after the non-socialist parties had won the national elections of September 1981. The new government was supported by the two other non-socialist parties, the Center Party and the Christian People's Party, which, together with the Conservative Party, hold on absolute majority.
During the summer of 1983, the Willoch government was enlarged by representatives of the two "supporters", and thus became a majority government.

Robert A. Bauer

The Brookings Institution, Washington D.C.

The United States and the European Neutrals

1. Introduction

The first part of this paper will deal with definitions and perceptions of the various concepts of neutrality and of the foreign policies of the European neutrals.

The second part will briefly recall the US neutrality experience.

In the third part, the US relationship with the four European neutrals will be reviewed.

In the fourth part, conclusions and observations will be submitted that might prove to have some usefulness in achieving deeper mutual understanding and in formulating concrete action programs.

2. Definitions and Perceptions

They vary, as shown by the following examples:

Former Austrian Vice-Chancellor Dr. Fritz Bock writes that Austria conducts an active neutrality policy; Sweden, as she implements her foreign policy now, never hesitates to take definite stands on events in other countries; Switzerland's neutrality can be considered an absence of policy[1].

Dr. Hanspeter Neuhold, Professor of International Relations and International Law at the University of Vienna, states that Austria and Switzerland have permanent neutrality status; Sweden has permanent neutrality as a principle of her foreign policy but without having entered into any legal obligation to this effect; Finland's neutrality is asymmetric with a pro-Soviet bias[2].

Finnish Ambassador Björn-Olof Alhom says that Finland's foreign policy can be considered a discreet neutrality policy[3].

American political scientist Dr. Joseph J. Kruzel describes Austria's neutrality as nominal, Finland's as bounded, Sweden's as active, and Switzerland's as passive[40].

Other Amercian perceptions will be cited in the last two parts of this paper.

3. The US Neutrality Experience

The origin of the US neutrality policy can be found in George Washington's Proclamation of 22 April 1793, at the time of the war between France and Austria, Prussia, Sardinia, Great Britain and the United Netherlands. It is noteworthy that the word neutrality is nowhere used. The Proclamation stated that "the duty and interest of the United States require that they should with sincerity and good faith adopt and pursue a conduct friendly and impartial toward the belligerent powers[5]".

Of subsequent neutrality legislations I cite the following two, which show the flexibility of the neutrality policy, conforming to changing world events and to Amercian public opinion:

Disillusionment with the results of American participation in the First World War, growing throughout the 20s, was aggravated by the depression as well as by the continuation of the "old diplomacy" in Europe, and deepened by the findings of the Nye Committee on Munitions Manufactures and by a host of books and articles arguing the desirability of isolation. The outbreak of the Italo-Ethiopian conflict in May 1935 led to the hasty passage of the Joint Resolution of 31 August 1935, designed to prevent US involvement in any international conflict. The following year Congress strengthened this Act by prohibiting loans to belligerents, and in January 1937 it took cognizance of the problem presented by civil wars by forbidding the export of munitions for the use of either of the opposing forces in the Spanish Civil War. Finally on 1 May 1937 a Joint Resolution reiterated these earlier resolutions, strengthening them in some particulars and giving larger discretionary powers to the President. A notable characteristic of this Neutrality Act was its failure to distinguish between aggressor and victim nations. Section 4 of the legislation mandated an exception to the effect that the Act should not apply to an American Republic or Republics engaged in war against a non-American State or States, provided the American Republic was not cooperating with a non-American State or States in such war[6].

The outbreak of the Second World War in September 1939 and the widespread sympathy for England and France forced a reconsideration of the Neutrality Act of 1937. On 23 September 1939 President Franklin D. Roosevelt appealed to Congress so to amend the existing neutrality laws as to permit belligerents to purchase and remove, at their own risk, war munitions and materials. After a long and bitter debate Congress defeated the isolationist forces and agreed to the "cash and carry" system, retaining, meanwhile, most of the safeguards of the earlier legislation[7].

4. US Relations with the Four European Neutrals

a) Austria

The US government signed the Moscow Declaration of 1 November 1943, which called for the re-establishment of an independent Austria, a victim of Nazi aggression. After the war, the US strongly supported the economic restoration of the Austrian Republic through the Marshall Plan, and worked for the end of the Four-Power occupation and for the re-establishment of full Austrian sovereignty, which was achieved on 15 May 1955, when France, Great Britain, the USA and the USSR signed the Austrian State Treaty. On 26 October 1955, the day after the date on which the last foreign soldier had to have left Austrian soil, the Austrian parliament passed a constitutional amendment committing the country to permanent neutrality.

Austria's active participation in UN affairs, in the UN peacekeeping forces, Vienna's role as the third UN city after New York and Geneva, and as host to two US-USSR summit meetings, her participation in OECD and EFTA—all these factors have earned Austria high respect in the United States. The personality and policies of former Chancellor Dr. Bruno Kreisky played a significant role in Washington's appraisal of Austria's foreign policy. In his book "White House Years", former Secretary of State Henry Kissinger describes Dr. Kreisky as shrewd and perceptive, who „had parleyed his country's formal neutrality into a position of influence beyond its strength, often interpreting the motives of competing countries to each other. His comments on trends and personalities were invariably illuminating. He had far more geopolitical insight than many leaders from more powerful countries. One of the asymmetries is the lack of correspondence between the abilities of some leaders and the power of their countries. (Prime Minister Lee Kuan Yew of Singapore is another good contemporary example.)[8]"

Two years ago an American official sounded a dissenting note from the generally positive view held in the United States of Austria's neutrality policy. In a speech before the Political Academy of the Austrian People's Party on 24 May 1982, Ambassador H. Eugene Douglas, Coordinator of the US Government for Refugee Affairs, dealt with Austrian neutrality and presented the following views: After citing a speech by President Reagan at his alma mater, Eureka College in Illinois, in which he said that the Austrian State Treaty had been foremost a product of Western unity, Mr. Douglas argued that Austrian neutrality would only endure if the foundation of Western democratic unity remained untouched. He then criticized the Austrian authorities for the handling of the visit of Libyan President Muammar Quadafi and of their relations with the PLO, as well as the attitudes of European socialists, among them Austrians, towards the US policy in El Salvador and Nicaragua. He warned against the replacement of a neutrality policy by a "policy of Neutralism", and finally took exception to Austria's commercial and financial dealings with the COMECON countries[9].

Official Washington made it clear that Mr. Douglas had expressed his own personal views and not those of the US government. While the speech drew much attention in Austria, it was ignored by the political and academic circles and the communication media in the United States.

b) Finland

At the end of 1982, the then Finnish Foreign Minister Per Stenbäk visited Washington and conferred with President Reagan and Secretary of State George Shultz. The Finnish Embassy in Washington informed me that the meetings were friendly and that no major problems arose. This good relationship was reaffirmed during the July 1983 visit of Vice President George Bush to Helsinki. In a dinner speech on July 2, Finnish Prime Minister Kalevi Sorsa, referring to the Finnish-American Bicentennial Festivities eight years ago whose motto was "old friends, strong ties," said: "This characterization describes in a perfect way the basic elements of the relations of our two countries[10]."

In his toast Vice President Bush said: "The United States fully recognizes Finland's unique position in the world and firmly supports your nation's neutrality. As you stated a moment ago, neutrality does not mean indifference, and we deeply appreciate Finland's efforts in the pursuit of peace. We feel particular gratitude for the recent deployment of Finnish troops in Lebanon as part of the United Nations Peacekeeping Forces, and we welcome the Finnish role in the Conference on Security and Cooperation in Europe, born here in Helsinki, and now, we believe, progressing to a new and promising stage[11]." And in an interview with the widely circulated magazine U.S. News & World Report the Vice President said: "The Finns are fiercely neutral, but they are friends of the United States[12]."

c) Sweden

On the same page of the above-cited interview, Vice President Bush discussed his meetings in Sweden, which he called "very open—very much give-and-take. I came away very grateful to Prime Minister Olof Palme for giving us the opportunity to have that kind of exchange." The Vice President then recalled that in one of his statements or toasts he said: "We were friends—that we respected Sweden's neutrality but were friends." A Swedish newspaper carried an editorial claiming that the Vice President was compromising Sweden's neutrality by asserting that America and Sweden were friends. Subsequently, various leaders, including Prime Minister Palme, made it a point to tell Mr. Bush that the editorial was absurd, and they indeed do consider Americans friends.

During the October 1982 visit to Sweden by US Secretary of Defense Caspar W. Weinberger, a controversy arose about statements he was alleged to have made on Swedish neutrality. Upon arrival at the airport in Stockholm on October 15, Mr. Weinberger was told by media representatives that he was quoted as saying that he did not really know whether Sweden was neutral. He responded by saying, "Well, I think that that is not a correct statement. What I said was that Sweden, whose policy I know has been one of non-alignment leading to neutrality in war, had a longtime commitment to democracy. And that is an intellectual commitment and a philosophical commitment, and one that we in the US understand and respect. Just as we understand and respect the political policy of neutrality." On October 17, in an interview with Swedish TV Channel One, and in his departure statement on October 19, Mr. Weinberger reiterated his understanding of and respect for the Swedish policy of neutrality[13].

These recent events and an analysis of US-Swedish relations over the past forty years confirm a statement made by Christer Persson of the Swedish Embassy in Washington, D.C. In a letter of 10 June 1983, responding to my request for material on US-Swedish relations, he stated that contacts and relations between Sweden and the USA were quite extensive and complex.

In the Second World War, Swedish neutrality policy was questioned when the Swedish government permitted the transit of German soldiers on leave through Sweden during the first years of the war, and the transit of the so-called Engelbrekt Division from Norway via Sweden to Finland in the summer of 1941. And in his memoirs President Harry Truman writes: "In the last week of the war, the Swedish government accepted an Allied proposal that would have amounted to Swedish intervention. It was the Allied plan to attack the German forces in Norway through Swedish territory, but surrender of the German forces in Norway came as this operation was being planned[14]."

Former Swedish Ambassador Sverker Aström, in his brochure "Sweden's Policy of Neutrality", writes about the transit of soldiers of belligerents during the Second World War: "It was impossible to keep on saying that we pursued a consistent policy of neutrality and at the same time to deviate, albeit in single cases, from the rules of neutrality[15]." It should also be noted that, according to the Fifth Hague Convention of 1907, a neutral State has the obligation not to allow its territory to be used by a belligerent.

The Swedish government's criticism of US Vietnam policy led to a serious deterioration of official relations. The post of American Ambassador in Stockholm was left vacant beginning August 1972. Prime Minister Palme's harsh statement after the renewed bombing of North Vietnam in December 1972 caused the US government not to return its Chargé d'Affaires on leave in the United States to Stockholm and to refuse to accept the new Swedish Ambassador to the United States. At that time, Secretary of State-Designate Henry Kissinger promised to review US policy toward Sweden[16]. He turned out to be one of the outspoken critics of the Swedish policy at that time. In "White House Years" he writes that "in December 1972 occurred what became known as the Christmas bombing to step up military pressure on Hanoi to reach a settlement of the Vietnam War. As controversial as this action was at home, it elicited vocal foreign criticism abroad." He refers specifically to the Swedish government, which compared us with the Nazis, and in parenthesis he adds "that they, of course, had been neutral during the Second World War." He also noted the castigation by other governments, among them the government of Finland[17]. Referring to the controversy over the military coup in Chile eleven years ago, he states in his book "Years of Upheaval" that "Switzerland had extended some form of recognition to the Junta in Chile, whereas the socialist government of Sweden cut off aid to Chile within forty-eight hours of the coup, before its implications could possibly be known. Had it ever acted with such alacrity, or at all, against left-wing tyrants? Indeed, it had lavished aid on Hanoi throughout the Vietnam War and afterwards[18]."

The relations deteriorated to such an extent that the Swedish Information Service in the United States decided to commission a public opinion survey to provide a profile of the attitude and knowledge level of American adults about Sweden. The survey showed a generally positive attitude towards Sweden. Fewer than one American in ten believed that Sweden's opposition to US Southeast Asia policies was an expression of anti-American feelings. But Sweden ranked considerably behind Switzerland for being the best friend of the United States[19].

Washington is fully aware of the Swedish government's criticism of US policy in Central America, to wit the speech by Swedish Foreign Minister Lennart Bodström before the General Assembly of the United Nations on 15 October 1982 in which he said: "It is obvious that a foreign power, the United States, plays a crucial role when it comes to keeping tottering dictatorships on their feet[20]." When this drew criticism from the Swedish opposition and from an American UN official, Prime Minister Palme, in a *Riksdag* (Parliament) debate on 15 March 1983 called this "a simple and true statement of fact[21]." On the same day, a statement of government policy was presented at the *Riksdag* which criticized the repression of a democratically formed trade union movement in Poland, the human rights situation in Turkey, Israel's invasion of Lebanon, Soviet "ruthless" violation of a small nation's sovereignty (Afghanistan), Vietnamese policy in Kampuchea, the *apartheid* regime in South Africa, and the "illegal" occupation of Namibia[22].

This policy substantially differentiates Sweden from the other European neutrals. Former Austrian Vice-Chancellor Dr. Fritz Bock defines it as follows: "According to the Austrian interpretation, neutrality includes, for example, Austria's obligation to refrain from interfering in the internal policies of other nations. This is a clear difference from Swedish neutrality, as it was implemented until the end of the period of socialist government in Sweden; Sweden never hesitated to take very definite stands on events in other countries[23]."

d) Switzerland

During the Second World War, the highly respected American writer and political philosopher Walter Lippmann called Switzerland "the most ancient republic in the Western world[24]." In an article in the New York Herald Tribune of 26 January 1943 he praised Switzerland's attitude "in the darkest hours of 1940 when only Great Britain's heroism and the blind faith of free men in the rest of the world stood between Hitler and Europe." On the other hand, the US government felt that Switzerland could have reduced its exports to Germany without endangering its vital interests[25].

In 1962, the US government took the position that, while EEC could make some useful economic arrangements with the neutral members of EFTA, Austria, Sweden and Switzerland, it would be wrong to accord free access to the Common Market to any State that would not accept the Community's political commitments. Former US Under Secretary of State George W. Ball writes that Sweden, Switzerland, and Austria claimed that such commitments would compromise their neutrality, and says: "They wanted it both ways, demanding the commercial benefits of the Community without assuming its burdens. In my view, Sweden and Switzerland defined 'neutrality' to suit their own purposes." While impatient with the Swiss and Swedish governments, who "hid behind neutrality for their own benefits," Mr. Ball notes that, in spite of Soviet objections, Austria applied for "association" with EEC. He ends this part of his judgments by accusing Switzerland of stubbornness and of an "overly rigorous definition of neutrality[26]."

Except for these occasional disagreements, US-Swiss relations have been consistently friendly, and Switzerland is undoubtedly in the US official and public mind the classical country of neutrality both in international law and in its foreign affairs, attitudes, and practices.

5. Conclusions and Observations

The US official attitude toward the European neutrals has undergone a remarkable change. Moving swiftly from neutrality and isolationism, because of World War II and its aftermath, to a Big Power role with global political, economic, and military commitments, the immediate official Washington posture was characterized by John Foster Dulles' condemnation of neutrality as an "immoral and shortsighted conception." Leaving the question of morality aside, there were questions raised already during the war whether modern warfare and changing world conditions had not destroyed the effective independence of small States. This was the basic argument of E. H. Carr, who wrote in 1942: "The small country can survive be seeking permanent association with a great power[27]."

Post-war history proved these concepts and predictions wrong. The European neutrals not only safeguarded their independence (Austria regained it in 1955), but assumed an increasing role in international affairs within the framework of the United Nations, as hosts to summit meetings and international organizations and conferences, and as conduits for mediation, to name a few important functions. The statements of Vice President George Bush quoted in this paper, reflecting the views of a conservative and ideologically committed Administration, prove that the constructive role of the European neutrals in international affairs is understood and appreciated in US government circles.

The American Ambassador to the United Nations, Jeane J. Kirkpatrick, a leading member of what are called the neo-conservatives, wrote: "It (the Reagan Administration) is willing to respect neutrality and non-alignment and to deal with nations outside the framework of East-West relations." She then says that the Reagan Administration stands ready to deal with non-aligned nations, on their own terms outside the East-West framework, and adds „wherever Soviet expansion has not made those nations a part of the East-West balance of forces[28]."

And Henry Kissinger makes the following assessment of the policies of non-aligned countries in connection with his discussion of Marshall Tito and his policies: "We recognize that it's (Yugoslavia's) policy of non-alignment, like India's, reflected a cold analysis of its self-interest. The serious non-aligned countries—not those which, removed from all danger, traffic in slogans—seek to cultivate the margin within which they can manipulate the international equilibrium. They will not hazard their security or well-being in quixotic gestures against us (unless tempted to do so by American supineness or sentimentality). Nor will they run the risk of becoming too closely associated with us no matter how 'understanding' of their proclamations our policy may be. Paradoxically, if we approach too closely, they will have to move away; as we distance ourselves they will have to move toward us; that is the almost physical law of non-alignment. In short, we did not succumb to the sentimental illusion that non-alignment resulted from specific grievances or misunderstandings. But we paid the non-aligned, and most particularly Yugoslavia, the compliment of recognizing that they were conducting a serious policy. Yugoslavia could not be won by accepting its rhetoric nor could it be permanently antagonized when we defended our own interests[29]."

In preparing this paper, I noted Joseph J. Kruzel's observation in the above-cited statement of research project that "it is surprising that analyses have not paid more attention to the concept of neutrality." This also applies to American public interest and opinion. Little attention was paid by the US media to Vice President Bush's visit to Finland and Sweden. Typical was the headline on p. A14 in the Washington Post of 12 July 1983: BUSH MAKES FEW WAVES AT HOME, CREATES BIG SPLASH IN SCANDINAVIA.

Part of the problem lies in the fact that the American public is practically overwhelmed on a daily basis by the news of crises in all four corners of the globe. Also, on this vast continent regional interests in world affairs vary considerably and often concentrate on foreign area developments of immediate concern to the region. There is a limit to the attention span of nations, as there is of individuals.

Another aspect of the American political scene is the role of the so-called ethnic lobbies—Greek-American, Polish-American, Hispanic-American, the pro-Israeli lobby, and others—who often exercise some influence on the formulation and conduct of US foreign policy. This does not apply to the US citizens who list their ancestry as follows:

Austrian	1,070,000
Finnish	616,000
Swedish	4,886,000
Swiss	1,228,000
General Scandinavian	340,000[30]

In his toast at the Finnish State Dinner, Vice President George Bush recalled the "Scandinavia Today" celebrations of 1982, attended by hundreds of thousands of Americans. One Finnish choir captivated an audience of some 60,000. The Finnish National Opera achieved a triumph in New York. There are, of course, other cultural and civic events sponsored by Americans of Austrian, Finnish, Swedish, and Swiss descent, but there is no evidence of any attempt to influence the US government or public opinion in political terms.

Public opinion plays an important role in the conduct of US foreign affairs. As pointed out earlier, the Swedish Information Service in the United States recognized this at the time of serious tensions between Stockholm and Washington, and conducted a large-scale public opinion poll. The role of the European neutrals in the service of security and peace deserves wider appreciation by the American public and by academic circles than is the case now. Probably few Americans are aware of the quiet, important role a European neutral statesman can play in international affairs, as described in the previously cited Henry Kissinger assessment of Dr. Bruno Kreisky's statemanship. A neutral country's influence on American public opinion will depend largely on the public's perception of that country's neutrality posture. I believe that the "ideal" neutral, best equipped for action in the interest of peace, is the one defined by President Woodrow Wilson in his "Appeal for Neutrality" in August 1914: "A Nation fit beyond others to exhibit the fine poise of undisturbed judgement, the dignity of self-control, the efficiency of dispassionate action; a Nation that neither sits in judgement upon others nor is disturbed in her own counsels and which keeps herself fit and free to do what is honest and disinterested and truly serviceable for the peace of the world[31]."

In the same vein, and especially applicable to the European neutrals, Martin Wight of the Royal Institute of International Affairs in London wrote in 1949: "Not burdened with particular concrete interests, small powers are able to be conscious of a universal interest[32]."

Notes

1 Fritz Bock, Austrian Neutrality, in: Robert A. Bauer (ed.), *The Austrian Solution: International Conflict and Cooperation* (Charlottesville 1982), pp. 157.
2 Hanspeter Neuhold, Permanent Neutrality and Non-alignment: Similarities and Differences, in: Bauer (ed.), op. cit., pp. 167.
3 Björn-Olaf Alholm, Finnland's Neutralitätspolitik in den achtziger Jahren, 3 West-Ost-Journal (1982), p. III.
4 Josef J. Kruzel, Statement of research project (summary) "Neutrality in World Politics", proposed chapter outline.
5 Henry Steele Commager (ed.), Documents of American History (6th ed., New York 1958), pp. 162.
6 Commager (ed.) op. cit., pp. 558, 560.
7 Commager (ed.) op. cit., pp. 600.
8 Henry Kissinger, White House Years (Boston 1979), p. 1204.
9 Eugene H. Douglas, Speech before the Political Academy of the Austrian People's Party (German text supplied by the Austrian Embassy, Washington, D.C).
10 Kalevi Sorsa, Speech, 2 July 1983 (text supplied by the Finnish Embassy, Washington, D.C).
11 George Bush, Statement (toast), 2 July 1983 (press release, Office of the Vice President, 2 July 1983), p. 1.
12 George Bush, US News & World Report, 25 July 1983, p. 32.
13 Caspar W. Weinberger, Statements provided by the US Department of Defense.
14 Harry S. Truman, Memoirs (vol. 1: Years of Decision, New York 1955), p. 203.
15 Sverker Aström, Sweden's Policy of Neutrality (Stockholm 1983), pp. 13.
16 US Congress, House, Hearing before the Subcommittee on Europe of the Committee on Foreign Affairs, 93rd Congress, First Session, 12 September 1973, p. 2. Cited as House Hearing.
17 Kissinger, op. cit., p. 1453.
18 Henry Kissinger, Years of Upheaval (Boston 1982), pp. 408, 413.
19 House Hearing, Study on American Attitudes toward Sweden, p. 12.
20 Lennart Bodström, Speech before the General Assembly of the United Nations, 15 October 1982, p. 11 (text provided by the Swedish Embassy, Washington, D.C).
21 Olof Palme, Speech at the *Riksdag* debate, 16 March 1983, p. 6 (text provided by the Swedish Embassy, Washington, D.C.).
22 Statement of Government Policy presented at the *Riksdag* debate on Foreign Affairs, 16 March 1983, pp. 3 (text supplied by the Swedish Embassy, Washington, D.C).
23 Fritz Bock, op. cit., p. 157.
24 Walter Lippmann, The Case of Professor R., New York, 30 June and 4 July 1942.
25 Edgar Bonjour, Geschichte der schweizerischen Neutralität, Band V 1939—45 (Basel 1970), p. 366.

26 George W. Ball, The Past has Another Pattern: Memoirs (New York 1982), pp. 219.
27 E. H. Carr, Conditions of Peace (New York 1942), p. 58.
28 Jeane J. Kirkpatrick, The Reagan Phenomenon and Other Speeches on Foreign Policy (Washington, D.C. 1983), pp. 9, 16.
29 Kissinger, op. cit. (footnote 8), p. 929.
30 Andrew Hacker (ed.), US, A Statistical Portrait of the American People (New York 1983), pp. 46.
31 Woodrow Wilson, Appeal for Neutrality, Message to the US Senate, August 1914, in: Commager (ed.), op. cit., p. 277.
32 Martin Wight, Power Politics (London 1949), p. 50.

Viktor A. Kremenyuk

Institute for the USA and Canada, Academy of Sciences of the USSR, Moscow

The European Neutrals and Soviet-American Relations

1. Introduction

The group of neutral and non-aligned countries in Europe includes States with different historical backgrounds, different social systems and political institutions. On the one hand, this group consists of such traditionally neutral States as Switzerland and Sweden, whose more than a century old neutrality has gained international recognition during two World Wars. This group has lately grown because some small States—Liechtenstein, Monaco, San Marino—and Ireland as well as Austria have resolutely opted for neutrality after the Second World War. But on the other hand, this group includes also such non-aligned States as Finland, Yugoslavia, Cyprus and Malta, which economically and socially are very different from the above-mentioned States. The differences are evident but, nevertheless, it is possible to speak about all these States as a single group, especially when assessing their role in European and world politics.

The role of the European neutral and non-aligned countries in international relations in general and in European politics in particular has been continuously increasing in recent years. The general process of universalization of international relations, including their democratization, the increasing ability of small and middle powers to influence world politics, opened the possibility for all European countries to contribute actively to the solution of the problems of the continent. Without undermining the existing alignment of forces in world affairs, this permitted the European neutral and non-aligned nations to take some useful and positive initiatives, which in some ways contributed to the stabilization of *détente* and the development of cooperation in Europe.

The central part in this process, of course, is played by the members of two world systems—NATO and the Warsaw Treaty. Achievement of approximate parity in the balance of their forces, both nuclear and conventional, has established a solid base for *détente* on the European continent, which led to the well-known agreements of the 1970s. The development of this process was influenced significantly also by such factors as the necessity to strengthen the territorial and political realities of post-World War II Europe and the objective need for stable political, economic, scientific and cultural relations between all parts of Europe.

And since this process is objectively in the interests of all European States, it made possible an increase in political initiatives by neutral and non-aligned nations, because in the process of *détente* and cooperation, more likely than in any other, all countries can positively participate on an equal basis in the solution of the problems of security and cooperation, if they have the desire and political will to do so.

Thus, with the development of *détente,* the European neutral and non-aligned States have come into the limelight of world politics (and not just as objects) and declared their positions, which appeared to have a significant place in the system of international relations, especially on the European continent. These interests could not but influence the relations between the Great Powers.

2. The State of Soviet-American Relations

The relations between the Soviet Union and the USA today—as during the entire period after the Second World War—are playing a central role in world affairs. The following features are characteristic of these relations at present:

a) Since 1980 the foreign policy doctrine of the US government (presented at that time as the "Carter Doctrine") proclaimed a policy of "Cold War" and confrontation with the Soviet Union. Any objective observer will agree that the events which prompted the "Carter Doctrine"—the situation in Afghanistan and Soviet assistance to the friendly revolutionary government in that country—were used simply as a pretext for the declaration of an aggressive global anti-Soviet policy by the US government. The decisions of late 1979 (NATO's "dual track" decision and the US Administration's simultaneous indifference to the attacks on the SALT II agreements in the US Senate) showed that, due to some failures of its own foreign policy, and first of all because of the inability to support the Shah regime in Iran, the Carter Administration gave in to the pressure of the right conservative wing of the American political spectrum and made an attempt to gain popular support through a chauvinistic turn in its foreign policy.

b) The new US Administration, which came to power in 1981, has significantly contributed to a further worsening of US-Soviet relations. Its position on US-Soviet relations is very similar to that of the American Administration of the 1950s, when the "Cold War" policy had reached a climax. The Reagan Administration not only attempted to reduce US-Soviet ties to a minimum and to speed up the arms race, but chose a sharp and "non-parliamentary" anti-Soviet rhetoric, which made the situation even worse and more complicated. Military programs of the present Administration for many years ahead make the perspective of a new spiral of the arms race very realistic, while the negotiations between the US and USSR—on the limitation and reduction of strategic arms, on intermediate-range nuclear forces in Europe, and on the mutual reduction of armed forces and armaments in Central Europe have been broken off after NATO started to deploy new INF systems in Western Europe.

c) The US Administration has considerably increased military and diplomatic pressure on some countries in Asia, Africa and Latin America that receive Soviet support and assistance. The leading figures of the American government are outspoken in threatening a "global offensive" against the Soviet Union and friendly countries, and do not exclude the possibility of using military force for this purpose.

d) The European continent is becoming an area of particularly high tensions. The US Administration is going ahead with its plans to deploy its intermediate-range nuclear weapons (Pershing 2s and GLCMs) in West European countries. This is posing a direct threat to the security of the Soviet Union and its allies.

These and some other aspects of US foreign policy, accompanied by insults and derogatory remarks by the President himself, his close associates, US mass media and some members of the Congress, create a high level of tension not only in US-Soviet relations but in the world arena as a whole. A situation of self-perpetuating conflicts has emerged, which is not immune to sliding into more dangerous stages of confrontation. This conclusion can be supported by several observations.

First, the general atmosphere of hostility, suspicion and total lack of mutual understanding created by the US Administration in US-Soviet relations has considerably reduced any possibility of bilateral consultations in situations fraught with potential conflict and threatening international peace and security. Due to the policy of the White House, the key elements of such important agreements as that on the Basic Principles of US-Soviet Relations (1972) and the Agreement on the Prevention of Nuclear War (1973) are factually inoperative. Any incident, as is shown by the story of the provocative overflight of Soviet airspace by the South Korean airplane, is immediately used not for seeking mutual understanding and conciliatory respect for the legal interests of the other side, but for increasing anti-Soviet propaganda and pushing new programs of nuclear and conventional armaments through the Congress. As a result, the danger of a conflict by misunderstanding or due to provocative actions of interested parties (*"agent provocateur"* scenario) has greatly increased.

Second, the situation in some regions of the Third World which for many years have been treated by Washington as areas for its "showdown" policy has also worsened. Very dangerous situations, which could lead to major open conflicts, exist in and around Nicaragua, Lebanon, Syria, Angola. Among the key factors, which could contribute to bringing these conflicts to the level of international crisis, are:

— the growing role of countries and regimes supported by the aggression committed by the United States and Israel against Lebanon in June 1982; the contemptuous position adopted by South Africa, which has refused to carry out UN decisions on Namibia's liberation and has been supported in this policy by the US Administration; escalation of interference in the internal affairs of El Salvador and Nicaragua by Honduras and Guatemala—all this leads to a sharp increase in local and regional tensions;

— due to a deadlock in Great Power cooperation, the possibilities of international peace-making have considerably decreased at the same time. This can aggravate further the situation in some strategically important areas. The war between Iran and Iraq threatens to cut oil transport lines in the Persian Gulf area and thus could produce a major world crisis.

Each of the above-mentioned events can cause a negative resonance in US-Soviet relations, both as a result of confrontation sought by the Reagan Administration and of its possible unilateral actions including military intervention, which becomes more possible with the increase of US military presence in the Third World (especially in the Middle East).

Third, after about a dozen years of peaceful development, Europe can be again submerged in the danger of "Cold War" policies. The deployment of US intermediate-range nuclear weapons on the continent will not only contribute to higher tension due to the above-mentioned reasons, but will, in addition, create a situation of high unpredictability and instability, since the threat of a first, disarming strike against the territory of the Soviet Union will become very plausible. The danger of crises due to misunderstanding, miscalculation or provocation will inevitably increase.

In this dangerous situation, which is acknowledged everywhere, the still existing communication channels between the two countries, including international fora where the urgent problems of peace and security are discussed, e.g. the CSCE process and the Vienna negotiations, have become considerably more significant. And, since a stalemate in US-Soviet relations produced by US policy does not permit us to expect any positive breakthrough at these negotiations through joint Soviet-American actions, additional stimuli and possibilities arise for the initiatives of neutral and non-aligned countries, if these initiatives are prompted by the desire to strengthen peace, develop *détente* and not to seek unilateral advantages detrimental to the interests of the others. It is even possible to say that in this situation the responsibility of neutral countries in the field of security and stability in Europe has increased considerably. Concern about these matters is displayed both in governmental and public opinion sectors in these countries.

The objective conditions for the initiatives of neutral States do exist; they depend on some more fundamental trends in European politics during the last decade.

3. The "Europeanization" of European Politics

The "Cold War" period of the 1950s left behind a lot of negative results: relations characterized by hostility and suspicion; the arms race; the division of the world into military blocs etc. Among these results was also the fact that the political initiatives of States which potentially could have contributed significantly and positively to world developments were completely or partially paralysed; their scope was limited to specific problems or specific issues only. This was one of the consequences of "bipolarity" in international relations which resulted from the logic and practice of the "Cold War".

It is quite sufficient to remember the story of the confrontation between the Eisenhower-Dulles Administration with the Non-Aligned Movement. The concept of this movement was laid down in the late 1940s, but only in the 1960s, when the first easing of tensions began, could this movement start its organizational activity, and only in the 1970s could it proclaim its interests.

A similar fate was assigned to the neutral and non-aligned States in Europe. The governments of these countries have managed to resist tremendous pressure by Washington and those in Western Europe who continued to think in terms of a *"cordon sanitaire"* around the Soviet Union. Nevertheless, these countries have managed to preserve their sovereignty and the right to choose their political orientation and not to join military blocs. But the price they paid was rather high: In Europe, which was divided into military blocs, their political role became negligible.

Meanwhile the desire of Atlantic circles to create a division in Europe, to pit different European States against each other in the name of anti-Communism and anti-Sovietism, had some far-reaching consequences. In particular, this policy has reduced Europe's traditionally important political role in the international system and thereby helped to achieve at least two objectives:

— to fill the vacuum left after the European role in world politics had been weakened, by the role played by USA;

— the substitution of the American (or "Atlantic") concepts for the European concepts of European politics.

The "Cold War" atmosphere and artificial subdivision of the continent permitted to achieve those goals. A sharp cleavage appeared in the relations of the two German States. The traditionally close Soviet-French and Polish-French relations were drastically curbed. Even the relations between such traditionally good neighbors as Austria, Hungary and Czechoslovakia were practically severed. This partition of Europe, the intense hostility between its two main parts, enabled the USA not only to impose on the West European countries (and not only on the members of NATO) its own understanding of European politics, but also to create a totally new alignment: "Atlantic Europe" against the rest of the continent. The position of the European neutrals became very unstable and their political role negligible at that time.

This new alignment in Europe was sometimes rather logically explained by American and West European Atlantic circles since its foundation was anti-Communism and anti-Socialism. But is could not eliminate the historically strong political, economic and cultural ties among European nations. For hundreds of years Russia was closely tied to Western Europe. It had close political relations with it in past centuries and during the Second World War. Russia had always been an integral economic part of Western Europe and played the role of its agricultural and raw materials supplier in the 18th, 19th and early 20th centuries. Cultural and ideological ties were always very strong among all European nations.

The abnormality, from the historical and all other points of view, of the political situation in a divided Europe could not be a foundation for a long-term policy. There appeared factors even during the "Cold War" which tended to put an end to this abnormality. And when in the 1960s the "Cold War" situation started to fade away, these factors came to the fore, first dominating France's foreign policy, then the *"Ostpolitik"* pursued by the social-democratic and liberal government of the Federal Republic of Germany.

Among these factors the following can be mentioned:

— an understandable desire of the European nations to accept the results of World War II; to eliminate the possibilities for unsolved problems of that period to become sources of new conflicts; to lay the foundations of a new period of European history, which was made impossible by the "Cold War";

— an objective need to "Europeanize" European politics, to make them less dependent on US global designs, which tended to include Europe among the possible areas of US-Soviet confrontation. The Eurocentric cultural and political tradition was simply insulted by such an approach;

— a logical demand to put an end to artificial barriers established by the "Cold War" situation. The interests of economic growth, especially of the countries which had lost their colonies, resistance to spiritual American domination and rather sober aspirations to end high tensions on the continent—everything demanded a new European (as opposed to the "Atlantic") approach.

The dominant trend which resulted from these factors has been the "Europeanization" of European politics, which is supported by many governments and influential public circles. This wide notion usually encompasses different insights and aspirations, among them the understanding that there is only a common future for the peoples of Europe, though their differences in ideologies and policies will continue to exist; the justifiable desire to avoid a repetition of the tragic events of World War II, which, if unleashed, would be further aggravated by the use of weapons of mass destruction; the possibility to utilize, for everyone's benefit, the existing division of labor and geographical distribution of raw materials on the continent; finally, a very understandable desire not to become an object of global competition, and even a widespread mood to put an end to years of dependent existence under the American "umbrella".

These considerations have played a visible role in the success of CSCE. Though these ideas sometimes are supported by parties and groups which stand on different sides of the political spectrum, and sometimes the ideas themselves sound very different (from "pan-European" to "European chauvinism"), the general trend to "Europeanize" European politics has become a very influential element of the whole process. It is impossible to understand the interaction of political forces on the continent without due regard to this phenomenon.

4. The Role of the Neutral and Non-Aligned States of Europe

The development of the political situation in Europe is influenced by various circumstances. Trends toward "Europeanization" are accompanied by reinforcing or opposite processes.

The European Socialist countries have proposed their constructive program of further development of the process of European security and cooperation. This program has to get to the minds of people through relics of the "Cold War", through anti-Communist prejudices and fears born out of years of propaganda. The major points of this program were laid down in the declarations of the Political Consultative Committee of the Warsaw Treaty Organization in Moscow (1978), Warsaw (1980), and Prague (1983). In general, these points—the appeal to strengthen security and to promote disarmament, to establish a network of mutually beneficial cooperation in the fields of trade, scientific research, technology, culture and information—respond to the mood of public opinion and of the governments in many European States.

At the same time, European policies are influenced by opposite factors. The present concept of European policy endorsed by the US Administration can be summed up in just a few words: "European theater of war". This concept, which regards Europe and the European countries merely as a possible battle-field, is in essence a very dangerous scenario for Europe's future. Nevertheless, it is supported in those countries where conservatives are in power and in some countries with so-called socialist governments. Its apodictic wording influences those who try to stay in the middle, since it adds a crisis dimension to the whole sphere of East-West relations. Even the governments which assess their interest in survival more realistically have to follow the line of "Western solidarity".

The logical outcome of this situation is a lack of positive initiatives by European NATO members, especially if these initiatives do not to serve US interests. When US allies try to suggest some ambivalent initiatives which are designed to satisfy both their interests and those of the USA, they share the fate of the "dual track" decision, whose first compenent is in force, whereas the second (US-Soviet negotiations) is obsolete.

But European interests do not permit a vacuum in political initiatives, and this leads to an increased role of the neutrals.

Their attempts to formulate their own position on the problems of European security and cooperation undertaken earlier were ignored by Washington. Moreover, in the late 1960s the Atlantic circles in Western Europe launched a derogatory campaign (started, as some suggest, by Richard Löwenthal) against "Finlandization". It tended to discredit the independent moves by the European neutrals to suggest an acceptable concept for European policies.

But with the development of the conditions for the beginning of *détente* and with a growing understanding that the time had come for formulating a genuine European position on the future of the continent, the situation changed. In these circumstances, the neutral States could take several positive initiatives, from hosting important negotiations to chairing the final stage of CSCE in Helsinki. The international prestige and authority of the neutral States have increased considerably.

The main cause of this development is, of course, not a previous lack of initiatives regarding Europe's future. The genuine causes, at least the most important of them, are the following:

First, these initiatives respond to the spirit of the time and to the historical trend. The neutral States played a positive rôle in the success of the Madrid CSCE follow-up conference of the 35 signatories of the Helsinki Final Act. Finland and Sweden have suggested the denuclearization of Northern Europe. Sweden has proposed a 300 km wide "nuclear-free corridor" in Central Europe. Austria and other neutral States are outspoken in their support for arms control negotiations on limiting intermediate range nuclear weapons in Europe. All these positions are generally welcomed, since they respond to the need for enhancing security in Europe and reflect the spirit of responsibility for the future of the old continent.

Second, the neutral States are active in the field of developing mutually beneficial economic relations between East and West. They are against any political interference with this process. On May 31, 1983, Federal Chancellor Fred Sinowatz was very eloquent on this point. The neutral States benefit from these economic exchanges. This fact does not remain unnoticed in other European countries which suffer economic hardship.

Third, the neutral States, thanks to their status, represent a Europe not divided into hostile military blocs. The idea to eliminate military blocs in Europe has its most visible effect in the existence of these States.

This position of the neutral States attracts the attention of some NATO countries. Essentially, the position of Greece on a nuclear-free zone in the Balkans is very close to that of the neutrals. The governments of Norway, Denmark and Iceland are interested in the Finnish proposals supported by Sweden for a nuclear-free Northern Europe. The governments and public opinion of the "Scandilux" countries (Denmark, The Netherlands, Belgium and Luxembourg) have expressed an interest in the idea of a nuclear arms freeze in Europe.

The positions of the neutral States are supported by Social-Democrats in several European countries. In turn, this political movement, which is strong in neutral countries, proposes its own initiatives, not only regarding security in Europe, but also regarding problems of enhancing security in the Middle East, Central America and Southern Africa.

Thus, within the context of the positions of the European and the broader alignment of forces on most urgent problems—those of preventing a new World War and providing security, of stabilizing the international situation and of increased cooperation—a certain neutral position has been formed. In general, it responds to the need for positive solutions to the above-mentioned problems. This is an essentially new development in post World War II Europe. It can be explained both by a general trend in international relations toward more equitable participation by all States in finding solutions to the problems on which their fates depend and by a growing feeling of responsibility in these countries for the future of the continent. Such trends cannot but meet with a favorable response by those participants in world politics who are concerned over growing tensions resulting from the desire of the US Administration to achieve a position of strength.

This explains the context in which the role of the European neutrals in Soviet-American relations can be assessed. These relations, as was already mentioned, have been brought to a stalemate by the new US foreign policy. The only way out is through a return to *détente* and cooperation. But it would be naive to expect the present US Administration to be capable of such a return. Judging by its actions in the sphere of arms expenditures, in the field of negotiations (and not only with the USSR; e. g. the position of the Reagan Administration on the "global round" or its refusal to sign the new Law of the Sea Convention are quite significant), by its actions in Central America or in the Middle East, one can be sure that the most logical and acceptable policy for it is the increase of tensions, a return to the situation of "brinkmanship".

In this situation one can only expect the re-emergence of hostilities and confrontation. But this time this atmosphere will be aggravated by the deployment of US intermediate-range nuclear systems, which significantly undermine strategic stability and increase instability which may lead to crises on the continent. This adds to the prospect of a further deterioration of US-Soviet relations the dimension of a special danger for the European States. This fact was especially underlined in the declaration of the Secretary General of the CPSU Central Committee, the Chairman of the Presidium of the Supreme Soviet, Yuri Andropov. And even those who presently support the deployment of further US nuclear forces in Europe cannot realistically expect their security to be guaranteed thereby.

The members of the Atlantic Community try even now to label the foreign policy initiatives of neutral countries as a sign of "Finlandization". But it is evident that these initiatives gain moral authority and political significance since, in contrast to US sponsored NATO decisions, they are based on common sense and an understanding of strategic and historical realities. In a way, the European neutrals, particularly Sweden, Austria and Finland, speak for a large part of the peoples of Western Europe which is against the deployment of US nuclear weapons in their countries. This fact is not yet properly assessed in Washington, but in Western Europe, in NATO countries, the governments feel concerned about it.

The foreign policy activities of the European neutrals do not occur, of course, in a vacuum. They are related to the political positions of both political-military groupings in Europe, and may be strengthened or weakened by them. On the main problems of crucial importance to Europe they are now generally rather close to the views of the Socialist countries. And this is a very important development since it contributes to a new alignment in Europe which can bring about an estrangement between US policy and the positions of a large part of the European population. The "Struggle for Europe" started by US Administrations with NATO's "dual track" decision in December 1979 can very well evolve into an anti-American mood of those Europeans who see a real danger to their future in the US "forward deployment" strategy.

For the context of Soviet American relations, such a turn of events could play a role similar to that of the US defeat in Indochina.

5. Concluding Remarks

Increased political activity by the neutral countries is evidence of the democratization of international relations and, at the same time, a factor which further accelerates this process. These initiatives are not always logical or consistent, for example, in the approach to "Superpower hegemony". But since they contribute to the solution of the main problem, that of security and cooperation in Europe, they can be regarded as a positive and constructive development in recent history.

In the present situation, when relations between the USSR and USA, due to the foreign policy line adopted in Washington, have become a possible source of tension, the role of the neutrals can become even more significant in the task of stabilizing *détente* in Europe, in avoiding the next steps in the arms race on the continent, and in the settlement of conflicts.

Recently the European neutrals proposed a series of initiatives: an intermediate-range nuclear weapons freeze, non-deployment of new arms of this type in Europe while the negotiations in Geneva were still in progress, and some others. It is quite prossible that their contribution to progress in international relations will become even more significant. In this respect, it is logical to expect them to play a positive role in strengthening peace in Europe and, in so doing, in stabilizing Soviet-American relations.

László Valki

International Law Department, Eötvös Loránd University, Budapest

Neutrality: A Hungarian View

1. Preliminary Remarks

The author of this paper, who is expected to outline the Hungarian view, is in a difficult position. The organizers of the conference have, no doubt, invited experts from various countries to hear from them many-sided and differentiated viewpoints in connection with the role of the neutral countries in preserving European peace and security. Beside the anticipated views of approval, the organizers would obviously welcome some critical remarks as well. But in the recent past, both official and non-official Hungarian public opinion have developed such a positive picture of the activities of the neutral countries and voiced practically such non-critical views that the following paper might perhaps look one-sided and biased; but I think it reflects the truth.

It is an interesting feature of the neutrality issue, at least for an international lawyer, that neither official nor non-official Hungarian public opinion distinguishes between the four countries as to whether they are legally bound to maintain their neutrality or not. The last time the legal aspects of neutrality were discussed was when Austria wanted to regulate her relations with EEC. It then became obvious that the specific obligations of neutrality can be interpreted so differently that their contents cannot be defined precisely. However, since these problems are not relevant any more, the legal aspects have no bearing on the subject any more. This, of course, does not mean that this problem may not surface again in case of some concrete issues in the future. Legal problems come up mostly when political conflicts arise among States. But since there is no such conflict at this moment between Hungary and any of the neutral countries in Europe, nobody is going to raise the legal aspects of neutrality. It can further be observed that the four countries are not conducting their neutral policies because they are under a legal obligation to do so but because such a policy appears to be in their basic internal or external political interest.

Although neutrality is originally a military conception, the military aspects of this status are not emphasized in recent dicussions in Hungary either. Naturally, we consider it highly favorable that no NATO troops are stationed in the immediate vicinity of the Hungarian frontiers; and we know, of course, that

Austria's Western neighbors also appreciate the fact that Warsaw Pact units are at a proper distance from them. Apart from this, military aspects have long been overshadowed by purely foreign policy, economic or cultural considerations, which is a clear sign of the fact that the beneficial effects of *détente* still exist.

What really matters now to the Hungarians, is that on the other side of the border between East und West there are some countries which—although unambiguously belonging to the West—consistently pursue a policy of national interest and not a policy furthering bloc interests, i. e. the interests of other States which are, for example, outside Europe, have a much larger population and incomparably larger military and economic capabilities. Such a policy could probably be considered a sign of healthy pluralism in international relations and undoubtedly contributes to the democratization of these relations. It is extremely important for us that we should not face a rigid, hostile bloc of capitalist countries. This fact makes it certainly easier to pursue our national interests, too, both in foreign and internal policies.

Apart from the above-mentioned considerations, the views of official or non-official public opinion in Hungary on the four European neutral States are determined mostly by bilateral factors. People are not inclined to generalize about the policies of the neutral countries as such; they prefer to draw conclusions from the actual policies of these countries in their bilateral relations with Hungary, from the level of cooperation they are ready to develop with us. As will be seen from this paper, this level is different from neutral country to neutral country.

2. Public Opinion

Non-official public opinion regarding the neutral States has always been highly positive. It is Austria that tops the list in this regard. The reasons can easily be understood. Due to geographic proximity and the common historical past, Hungarians have always had ample opportunity to get acquainted with the Austrian people and with the foreign policy of that country. Strangely enough, in the region East to the River Leitha, the past is evoking mostly positive memories, although schoolchildren, in their studies of the history of the 18th and 19th centuries, inevitably learn that the Hapsburgs conducted a policy of oppression and that the two most important Hungarian independence movements fought against the Hapsburgs (1703—1711, 1848/49). But as regards the grown-up population, the neighboring State evokes different memories. And this change is not merely due to the seven decades that have passed between the collapse of the Austro-Hungarian Monarchy and the present day, but it is also due to a new approach developed by the Hungarian economic historians in the last fifteen years.

In their studies of the Monarchy, these historians have pointed out that, in spite of political subordination, being part of the Monarchy had been far less unfavorable for Hungary than earlier judgments had concluded. This was particularly true of the period between the "Compromise" (*"Ausgleich"*) in 1867 and World War I. In the course of this period, there emerged possibilities for the development of a comparatively significant Hungarian processing industry. The Hungarian industrial products could find their market within the Monarchy, on a comparatively large territory. In addition, the same currency was used in all parts of the Monarchy. Consequently, the Hungarian economy never struggled with currency problems (in contrast to certain periods following Hungarian independence).

Tourism of the early 1960s also had a favorable impact on public opinion. In this period it first became possible for considerable numbers of Hungarians to travel to the West. Naturally, their first stopover was Austria. Breaking with the severe isolationist policies of the 1950s, the Hungarian government, having the necessary means at its disposal, supported this tourism. Since the Hungarians were cordially welcomed in Austria, this country received favorable ratings in Hungarian public opinion. The fact that the Austrian living standard was comparatively high also played a role. Thus Hungarian tourists travelling to Austria got acquainted with a friendly, stable State, whose economy was in good shape.

It must also be borne in mind that up to the recent past it was German that was the most widely spoken foreign language in Hungary—of course also due to Hungary's belonging to the Monarchy. Consequently, there were no serious linguistic obstacles to communication between the two nations.

A further essential factor is the positive image Austria enjoys in the Hungarian mass media. After getting beyond the conflicts of the years following 1956, there were practically no critical reports by the Hungarian press and radio on Austria. The Hungarian press is refraining from comments or critical remarks even in the case of unfavorable phenomena in Austria and is publishing only matter-of-fact information.

The neutral and independent policy of Austria, of course, also contributed to the development of a positive attitude. This policy was personified during the last years in Chancellor Bruno Kreisky, who enjoyed enormous popularity here. It became customary in Hungary to speak about the "K. u. K." (Kreisky und Kádár) relationship.

As far as Finland is concerned, impressions in Hungarian public opinion are likewise favorable. Although, due to geographical distance and for language reasons, relations with the Finnish people cannot be compared with those with the Austrians, Hungarians nevertheless cherish the kinship with the Finnish nation very vividly. Another important fact is the very warm welcome which Hungarian tourists have received in Finland. There emerged the feeling that Hungarian tourists were liked in Finland just because they were Hungarians. It would be difficult to find objective reasons behind this mutual affection. However, the foreign policy pursued by Finland since the Second World War has undoubtedly played an important role in this respect, too.

Probably Switzerland is in third place on the "popularity list". The favorable stereotype the Swiss enjoy in the world is also shared by Hungarians, who respect the Swiss as reliable, precise and diligent people. These are qualities which can earn a very high prestige for a people. This favorable image, however, is somewhat tarnished by the fact that, although foreigners visiting Switzerland are given a friendly welcome, it lacks the cordiality which other peoples show. Another shadow which falls on this favorable image is due to the fact that Hungarians have learned about the difficulties foreigners living in Switzerland have to cope with.

To Hungarian public opinion, Switzerland's internal policies are entirely unknown. Should a public opinion poll be taken today, Hungarians, in all probability, would fail to be able to name a single Swiss politician. Hungarians, however, regard Swiss neutrality with respect.

Sweden's image is similarly favorable. The high level of social security in that country is well known in Hungary. Opinions on social-democratic domestic policies—in spite of the fact that they are often accompanied by high taxes—are highly positive. Social democracy is among the concepts which enjoy the best resonance in Hungary. Beside Bruno Kreisky and Willy Brandt, Olof Palme, too, enjoys considerable popularity in Hungary.

Naturally, the positive opinions outlined above are not primarily or solely the result of the neutral policies pursued by the countries concerned, but, as I have already briefly indicated, other circumstances also play a role. The fact, however, that Hungarian mass media continuously present a highly favorable picture of these countries, is obviously related to the neutral policies they pursue. It is likewise due to their neutral policies that the public statements of the political leaders of the four countries do not contain any disapproval, at least in the last decade and a half, of Hungary.

It is an interesting feature of the over-all picture that has developed in Hungarian public opinion that ideological differences, namely the fact that all four countries have another type of social system, does not play an essential role in this regard. Even those parts of public opinion which declare themselves the most active adherents of socialism accept the above-mentioned countries with their different socio-political system. Even they do not feel that those differences can essentially influence the development of relations between peoples. An eventual reassessment of other non-neutral nations in Hungary would, in all probability, rank them without much attention to the fact that they belong to another social system. That international antagonisms and the relations between groups of countries belonging to two different social systems influence the subconscious attitude, is of course a different matter. Similarly, Western views on Hungary (or socialism) do not remain indifferent to such differences either.

3. Bilateral Relations

In the following analysis, factors that are not directly related to the policy of neutrality will again be discussed. On the other hand, neutrality is one of the determining factors in the development of bilateral relations as well. To the best of my knowledge, however, in these relations, especially in intergovernmental, diplomatic negotiations, little mention is made of neutrality itself. In most cases, contacts are established to tackle more concrete problems.

a) Austria

Our bilateral relations with Austria have become intensive and beneficial to both sides in the period following the "Second Compromise" *("Zweiter Ausgleich")*, after several years of international political tensions, that followed the events of 1956 in Hungary, had come to an end. The Austrian Foreign Minister Bruno Kreisky first visited Hungary in 1964. In 1965, this visit was returned by his Hungarian counterpart, János Péter. The first meetings between Heads of State took place in 1967—1969. However, as Federal Chancellor, Kreisky visited Hungary only as late as 1973. Another three years had to elapse until János Kádár received and accepted an Austrian invitation. Since then, however, meetings between the Heads of State, Heads of Government, and/or at the ministerial level have become more frequent and regular. In 1977, President Kirchschläger visited Budapest, while in 1979 Hungarian Head of State Pál Losonczi traveled to Vienna. We consider it very important that we recently had the opportunity to receive the new Austrian Chancellor, Fred Sinowatz, who paid his first foreign visit after he had succeeded Bruno Kreisky to Hungary. All these visits helped to intensify Austro-Hungarian relations. In Hungary, there is a very strong conviction that this process will continue in the years to come.

The same favorable assessment applies to the legally regulated relations as well. Among the bilateral treaties, the most important agreement concerns the abolition of the obligatory visa system. Other important treaties include consular, extradition, criminal-legal assistance, and cultural-scientific agreements, as well as an agreement on the equivalence of school certificates.

The present economic relations between the two countries are characterized by intensive trade. Our trade turnover with Austria is comparatively high. It is more than twice the turnover with the United States and one third of the turnover with the Federal Republic of Germany. This means an average 800 million dollars of total turnover; however, the Hungarian import share unfortunately secures only 60 to 80 per cent of this. It is for this reason that a free trade agreement with Austria would be important to Hungary. In 1976, it seemed that

Austria was ready to sign such an agreement with Hungary. Prime Minister György Lázár proposed to Bruno Kreisky to conclude a free trade agreement that year. The answer given by the Austrian Chancellor was that his government "would give favorable consideration to the proposal". This was also included in the joint communiqué issued on the talks between the two sides. In December 1976, however, during János Kádár's visit to Vienna, it became obvious that Austria was not willing to conclude an agreement along these lines, mainly because of alleged West German objections. This was all the more significant because Austria, as a member of EFTA and as a result of her free trade agreements with the European Communities, had become part of a big economic unit. Exports to this unit are causing increasingly serious problems for Hungarian foreign trade. It must be added here that Austrian tariff rates are higher than the rates of the West European countries or those of EEC. Trade with Austria is also somewhat hindered by the so-called countersigning *("Vidierungsvermerk")* procedure which was introduced allegedly as a protection against dumping prices. Although this procedure is a formal one, it undoubtedly belongs to non-tariff trade barriers. On the other hand, in some individual cases Austrian authorities are granting tariff concessions to Hungarian exporters.

In spite of these problems, the Hungarian appraisal of Austrian foreign trade policy is positive. Our Austrian partners belong to the most reliable and honest trade partners. Therefore, all our endeavors are aimed at extending economic relations. Nobody in Hungary now has reservations about Austria's above-mentioned free trade agreements with the European Communities. It was only in the early 1960s that a certain anxiety arose. At the time, there were speculations about the institutionalization of Austria's relations with West-European integration. The question of the interpretation of Austria's neutrality was raised. More specifically, the issue of whether this neutrality should go beyond the military sphere or not was discussed. It was the general conviction in Hungary that already in peace-time a permanently neutral State must follow a political line which guarantees that in case of armed conflict it can preserve its neutrality. In Hungary at that time the opinion was held that Austria's association with EEC was incompatible with her neutrality.

Although association does not yet mean "joining" EEC, and though formally it would not infringe Austria's neutrality, factually, however, it would. As part of EEC's customs union, the Austrian national market would practically be united with the market of the European Community. This in turn would result in further economic integration with the members of the Community, first of all with the Federal Republic of Germany. The over 50% share of Austrian foreign trade with EEC would in all probability increase further to the disadvantage of the East European countries. The dependence of the Austrian economy would considerably increase the influence of the governing bodies of the Community. At that time, some even raised the issue of the violation of the so-called *Anschluß* ban of the Austrian State Treaty (Art. 4), which, however, was an obvious exaggeration.

Later it was learned in Hungary with dissatisfaction that, since the mid-1960s, intensive negotiations had been held between representatives of EEC and the Austrian government. According to our information, by the time of the Italian veto on 30 June 1967, those negotiations had come to a stage where preliminary agreement had been reached on Austria's admission to the Common Market's customs union. This meant that Austria was ready to adopt EEC's external customs rates. What is more, under this agreement, she was to adjust her agricultural policy to that of the Common Market.

Naturally, all these events already belong to the past; I mention them only for the sake of historical truth. The change in the Hungarian attitude towards the free trade agreement since that time is partly due to a highly favorable change in Austria's foreign policy towards Hungary. But it is also a result of a considerable modification of the Hungarian approach to West European integration itself. At the end of the fifties and during the following years, the European Communities had been branded by the Hungarian press and also in some official statements simply as the European economic base of NATO. Later, however, Hungary accepted the existence of the Common Market as a "reality" and—especially in the framework of CMEA—has even shown readiness to enter into institutionalized relations with the European Community. It became obvious that the Community did not pose such a political danger to the development of East-West relations as had earlier been assumed.

Hungarian politicians and diplomats who are in personal contact with their Austrian counterparts have a favorable impression of them. In their opinion, Austrian politicians serve the national interest of their country in such a way that they are paying considerable attention to the interests of other European countries as well, in spite of the fact that some of them, Hungary for instance, belong to a different social system. A recurrent adjective in Hungarian statements about the relations between the two countries is "exemplary". This means that Austro-Hungarian relations might serve as a model for the relations between all countries which have different political systems. It is especially important to underline this fact since, as is widely known, the leaders of the ruling Austrian Socialist Party do not share at all the ideology of the Communist Parties. An incident characteristic of this position occurred when, during his 1973 visit, Mr. Kreisky refused to see Mr. Kádár at the Central Committee headquarters. Nor was Mr. Kreisky willing to enter into inter-party relations. Nevertheless, the visit was highly successful. Subsequently, the Hungarian side also respected the SPÖ's standpoint, according to which inter-State relations are to be distinguished from inter-party relations. It is interesting to note, however, that the Austrian People's Party (ÖVP) was ready to establish such relations. Its Secretary-General has already been to Hungary some time ago; its Chairman Dr. Alois Mock has just visited Hungary in January 1984.

This evolution leads to the conclusion, that Hungary, too, accepts the viewpoint that permanent neutrality does not mean neutralism and, as a consequence, the Austrian government cannot be expected to take a neutral stand on ideological issues. The democratic political system of Austria is respected in Hungary as well as is Austria's support for classical Western values. Hungary gladly takes cognizance of the fact that at the same time Austria respects the Hungarian political system and, in spite of the differences in the political systems of the two countries, is willing to maintain close and friendly relations with Hungary. It is my conviction that both nations benefit from this state of affairs in their bilateral relations and that it greatly contributes to the preservation of peace and security and to the improvement of the quality of life in this part of the continent, which has suffered from so many conflicts in the past.

b) Finland

In the past decades, Hungarian-Finnish relations have also developed very positively. Here, too, something similar to the evolution of Austro-Hungarian relations occurred after the tensions following the events of 1956 had ceased to exist. In 1963, Mr. Urho Kekkonen first visited Hungary. In 1969, the Finnish President visited Hungary again. Although Janos Kádár first visited Finland only as late as 1973, this was not a negative sign, since Hungarian-Finnish relations had been developing well as early as the second half of the 1960s. It is not necessary here to list all the highly intensive contacts between the two States in the past two decades. It is sufficient to recall that shortly after his election, President Koivisto visited Hungary as early as 1982, and Janos Kádár returned his visit already in 1983. The Hungarian press commented on this latter visit in superlatives and underlined the various manifestations of personal sympathy which developed between the two statesmen.

Finland is the other West European country that was willing to sign an agreement with Hungary on the abolition of obligatory visas (Hungary submitted similar proposals to several other Western countries, including neutral and non-aligned countries, but failed to get a positive response). The ten-year economic-industrial and technical-scientific agreements signed in 1974 are significant, as well as a treaty abolishing trade obstacles, which is practically a free trade agreement. In 1978, a bilateral treaty on abolishing double taxation and in 1981, an agreement on criminal police matters were concluded.

Unfortunately, owing to geographical distance and to the characteristics of the industrial structure of the two countries, economic relations between Hungary and Finland are less intensive than political relations. Hungarian foreign trade with Finland reaches only one fifth of the volume with Austria, despite the fact that there are no administrative obstacles whatsoever to hinder the development of foreign trade. Nevertheless, our foreign trade experts appreciate very much the high level of development in certain processing industrial branches (such as the paper industry) and are trying to increase the volume of Finnish imports.

Also due to geographical distance, and because of the high Finnish price level, each year only about 4,000—5,000 Hungarian tourists have been visiting Finland in the recent past. From Finland, a similarly low number of tourists, 19,000—20,000, has traveled to Hungary. On the other hand, an astonishingly high number of Finns is studying Hungarian, attending day-time and evening university courses. The number of Finns who are visiting the Hungarian Cultural and Scientific Center, founded in 1980 in Helsinki, is similarly high.

Like the relations established with their Austrian partners, relations between Hungarian and Finnish politicians and diplomats on different levels are truly exemplary. In Hungary, the opinion is held that these particularly fortunate relations between countries belonging to two distant regions of Europe have a positive effect on the overall security of Europe as well. It is otherwise of special importance for us that the political steps taken by the Hungarian government continuously meet with positive reactions from both Austria and Finland. It is evident that reactions in the neighborhood are always an essential factor for the development of the political strategy of a given country. Such favorable reactions are strengthening those tendencies in Hungary that have been taking shape in the course of more than a quarter of a century since 1956.

c) Switzerland

That Hungarian-Swiss relations are good, but not distinctly intensive, is due to Switzerland's special political system, her sophisticated federal structure. The interruption of relations in the period following 1956 lasted much longer than in the case of Austria or Finland. Only in the 1970s did the Swiss government agree to a *rapprochement* with Hungary. In 1978, Swiss Foreign Minister Pierre Aubert visited Hungary and the Swiss Finance Minister also came to Budapest. Two years later, then Foreign Minister Frigyes Puja returned the visit of his Swiss counterpart, and the Hungarian Ministers of Foreign Trade and of Finance also visited Switzerland.

In 1973, Hungary signed an economic agreement with Switzerland which, among other things, provided for the establishment of mixed committees. The existence of these committees contributed to the significant development of our economic relations—they are considerably more intensive than the political relations. In recent years, our foreign trade turnover with Switzerland has been the same as that with the United States. The products of Swiss industry, highly developed in certain fields, are much in demand in Hungary. At present some 100 co-operation agreements between Hungarian and Swiss companies are in force; in this regard, Swiss industry is in second place, following the Federal Republic of Germany. Unfortunately, Hungary did not succeed in reaching a balance in her economic relations with Switzerland either. Hungarian exports cover only 60—70% of the annual imports from Switzerland.

Due to the Swiss federal system, there is no inter-State cultural agreement between the two countries. However, agreements were concluded instead between the Swiss and the Hungarian Academies of Sciences and also between the Hungarian Cultural Institution and its Swiss counterpart, although only as late as 1980.

I am convinced that the political relations have reached the existing level only because the Swiss government does not maintain particularly active relations with the rest of the world in general. Swiss foreign policy does not aim at spectacular international initiatives. On the other hand, we hope that Hungarian-Swiss relations on different levels which were established in the past will continue for the benefit of both countries.

d) Sweden

Swedish-Hungarian contacts were the last to develop. The first (and only) high-level meeting took place only four years ago, when Deputy Premier József Marjai visited Stockholm. There are now plans for Olof Palme to visit Hungary in 1984. In addition, however, in recent years several Hungarian government members have visited Sweden and *vice versa*. That contacts are not particularly intensive reflects the fact that there are no open questions to solve in Swedish-Hungarian relations. Meetings between the two sides up to now have been highly successful. We are therefore entitled to hope that relations will further develop in the future.

In the economic field, the long-term trade agreement, signed in 1982, can be considered significant. Furthermore, mention is to be made of the agreement (signed also in 1982) which abolished double taxation, and of a legal assistance agreement signed in September 1983. The trade agreement removed several commercial obstacles between the two countries. However, the maintenance by Sweden of the import permit system against countries with a State monopoly in the field of trade still makes the economic relations somewhat difficult. Nevertheless, as in the case of Finland, geographical distance is the main reason why the volume of trade is not particularly high—the turnover between Hungary and Sweden is about the same as between Hungary and Finland.

As regards cultural relations, an agreement was concluded comparatively early. In 1969, an agreement was concluded between the Hungarian Institute of Cultural Relations and the Swedish Cultural Institute. In 1972, this was followed by a cooperation agreement between the Academies of Sciences of the two countries.

The relatively low level of tourism between the two countries is also related to geographical distance and to the high Swedish price level. In the past few years, some 6,000—7,000 Hungarian tourists visited Sweden, while the number of Swedish tourists to Hungary was between 30,000—32,000.

It must be remarked here that the Swedish system of granting visas is still lagging behind the Hungarian procedure (entry visas to Hungary are issued within 24 hours at our Embassies, while at border crossing points or at the airport entry visas can be obtained immediately). We would also welcome a bilateral consular agreement with Sweden.

4. Multilateral Relations

The role which the four neutral States are playing in securing peace and security in Europe is given a highly favorable appraisal in Hungary. All the efforts made by these States to this end, especially in the last decade, have been greeted with great satisfaction in Hungary.

It is hardly necessary to enumerate all the well-known initiatives taken by the neutral countries to further promote *détente.* Suffice it to say that we consider the steps taken by the neutrals—many times in cooperation with non-aligned States—to be a qualitative change in the post-World War II period of European history. In the course of the Geneva phase and the CSCE follow-up conference in Belgrade we had already welcomed the first signs of the joint activity by those countries. However, it was during the Madrid meeting that the neutrals gave events a decisive impetus. It is a general conviction in Hungary that without the activities of the neutral and non-aligned countries, the Madrid meeting would have been a total failure. Four years ago, at the start of the talks, for well-known reasons, antagonism between East and West had been so severe that in Hungary many people lost their hope for a successful conclusion of the meeting. The first draft of a final document by the neutral and non-aligned States was an enormous help to the common cause.

As is known, however, conflicts were not settled at that time, and a new text had to be drafted. According to our view, this latter draft gave another impetus to the deadlocked conference. Though the drafts were of a compromise nature, we still thought that they would serve the interest of the international community. The members of the "n+n" group drafted proposals not only on the basis of the lowest common denominator. Consequently, the Concluding Document of the

Madrid meeting does not merely report that the talks have eventually been concluded. The contents of this document provide a useful contribution to the development of European inter-State relations.

The members of the Hungarian delegation said that the representatives of the neutral States in Madrid had shown not only considerable good will and friendliness but very high professional competence too. In the course of the extremely difficult formal and informal negotiations, these representatives proved to be outstanding diplomats. Special appreciation was expressed for the heads of the Austrian and Swiss delegations, Mr. Ceska and Mr. Brunner.

It was observed by the participants of the Madrid conference that the neutral countries—which happened to belong to the smaller States of Europe—were looking for ways and means to take part in shaping the European political processes. Since Hungary does not belong to the bigger nations of Europe either, she followed these efforts with special satisfaction. According to our view, the participation of the neutral countries is not only significant from the point of view of their mediation activities, but also because they are making an important contribution to the democratization of international relations. It is clear that certain issues, such as the problems of strategic nuclear arms limitation, can only be solved by negotiations between the Great Powers. However, in practically all other fields, every State in Europe should participate in the solution of problems of common interest. Consequently, those institutional forms in which the smaller countries can express and represent their interests are highly important, especially because these countries have political and cultural traditions of their own and represent significant human values.

The recent changes in world politics gave rise to grave concern in Hungary, since she is keenly interested in maintaining *détente.* There is no room here for a deeper analysis of the causes that led to these changes. But it became clear that political processes within the United States had taken a turn unfavorable for us at the end of the 1970s. The trend of the development of these processes has been, however, influenced by the behavior of other States. In this regard, I think, the role the neutral countries have been playing in recent years must not be underestimated. Their foreign policy has probably demonstrated to the Carter and Reagan Administrations that not only the East European countries were interested in *détente,* but also the smaller States in the West.

Naturally, the foreign policy of the neutral countries was not solely intended to influence the policy of a Western power. In many cases, this foreign policy has affected the Socialist countries as well. Since the time we intensified our relations with the neutral countries, either in the course of the Madrid meeting or on the bilateral level, we, too, see a lot of things differently in this regard. For us, it is similarly important to clearly recognize the interests of the neutral countries to understand how they would like Europe to be, and what concrete political line they consider expedient on our part.

In addition to joint actions, we could witness, several times, beneficial individual steps by neutral countries as well. Some initiatives by one of the four States have met with very positive reactions in Budapest. We considered highly positive, for instance, the Kekkonen proposals regarding the creation of a Nordic nuclear-weapon-free zone, Bruno Kreisky's idea of linking European energy systems, Palme's suggestions to create a nuclear-weapon-free zone in the border areas of the two military alliances in Europe etc. It is not forgotten here that Vienna hosts the MBFR talks and several other meetings, and that the Austrian capital is going to host the next CSCE follow-up conference. Nor is it forgotten here that Finland provided facilities for the first and third phase of CSCE in 1973 and 1975, that Sweden is offering Stockholm as venue for the CSCE Conference on Confidence and Security Building Measures and Disarmament, nor that Switzerland—partly as one of the European centers of the United Nations—is the permanent host to various multilateral and bilateral negotiations. These host functions are obviously not limited to providing technical facilities; in addition, the diplomacy of the above-mentioned host countries has taken an active part in the preparation and organization of the meetings.

Other positive manifestations of the foreign policy of the neutral countries are also well known. It may be recalled here, for instance, that Sweden sharply condemned the US role in the Vietnam war and provided exile for US deserters and that Sweden had been the first Western country to support the new united Vietnam. Mr. Kreisky's efforts to help ease tensions in the Middle East are also positively evaluated by us.

There can of course be small differences in the foreign policies of the neutral countries. As neutrality is judged from Budapest, it does not mean any uniform foreign policy for all the four countries. In February 1982, for example, Austrian Foreign Minister Willibald Pahr, in his Madrid speech, condemned the sanction policy initiated and applied by some countries against Poland, while other representatives of the neutral States failed to denounce these actions. Another characteristic difference is to be noted in the interpretations by the neutral countries of the maintenance of the balance between East and West. In his speech at the opening session of the Madrid CSCE follow-up meeting, the Swedish delegate, for example, sharply criticized both "Superpowers", one for its role in Afghanistan, the other for its role in the Persian Gulf. At the same time, in his opening statement, the Finnish delegate abstained from concrete criticism of either of the Great Powers.

But whatever the differences are in the style of the foreign policies, we are absolutely sure that if the continuation of *détente* had depended solely on the neutral States, it could have easily been achieved.

Ljubivoje Aćimović

Institute of International Politics and Economics, Belgrade

In Search of Peace and Security: The Role of the European Neutrals. A Yugoslav Point of View

In the existing conditions of international relations characterized by a predominant role of the policy of reliance on force, along with an enormous accumulation and bipolar concentration of military power, it may appear at first sight as if there was hardly any role for the four European neutral States to play in search of peace and security. However, the experience acquired so far shows that the answer to this question is neither so simple nor negative. There is, indeed, some room for action for the neutral States in the field of promoting peace and security, just as the capabilities of the two Superpowers for action and influence are not unlimited. The whole complex system of interaction (between the two Superpowers along with their military alliances; within the alliances; between North and South etc.) puts certain limitations on the political potential of the most powerful States (as well as of others) in dealing with international affairs. This has been amply borne out by events, such as the Vietnam conflict, the Middle East crisis, the Iranian crisis, CSCE etc. Moreover, the whole history of the Non-Aligned Movement bears abundant evidence that a third-line (i. e. non-bloc) action, in contemporary international relations with the predominant bipolar structure of power, is not only possible but needed.

In other words, there is, no doubt, room for the European neutrals to make their contribution to promoting international peace and security. The question is only how large this room is, and how to use it to the best of these countries' abilities. And the next question that logically follows is to what extent and how successfully these countries have used this room for action so far.

Of course, one should not lose sight of realities and try to exaggerate the actual potential of the European neutral States, but, modest as it may be, their role is of importance and even in some situations particularly useful.

Before entering into a more specific discussion on the role of the European neutrals in search of peace and security, it may be useful to make a few preliminary observations. First, the nature of permanent neutrality in the post-World War II era is in fact rather different from that before 1945. The roots of this change lie in the "Cold War" and its effects (first of all, bloc divisions and a continuing confrontation between the two "belligerent" sides) which have made the status of permanent neutrality a factor of relevance in peace-time as well. Second, the role of the European neutrals and their practical contributions to peace and security have undergone quite an evolution during the period of *détente*. And third, these four European countries differ among themselves in many respects, including the origins, the character and the contents of their status and policy of neutrality, all of which has to be borne in mind when discussing this subject; but, at the same time, there are enough common features in the positions and policies of the European neutrals which justify a common treatment of their role in international relations.

The role of the European neutrals in peace and security promoting efforts can, for analytical purposes, be broken down into three components.

First, the position and the policy posture of keeping outside the two power blocs: At an earlier stage in post-war history, during the "Cold War", this was almost the only and, at any rate, the main function performed by neutral States in Europe with respect to peace and security. Thanks to the neutrality of these States and to the non-alignment of Yugoslavia, the European continent was not fully divided into spheres of influence and totally covered by bloc structures.This fact was and still is of manifold importance—strategic, political and psychological. As a result, the line of direct military confrontation between the two blocs has been interrupted; concrete evidence has been furnished in practice that independence and security can be ensured also on a non-alliance basis; the bloc-type policy has not been the only option left to European States. This European phenomenon of non-bloc policy (combining neutrality and non-alignment), however modest the size and power of these countries, has been of undoubted significance both during the "Cold War" and the period of *détente*.

Second, European neutral States play a rather important role in the field of good offices and mediation. They are in a good position to provide valuable assistance to other States, in particular in conditions of international conflict and rivalry. They make it easier for the States concerned to communicate with each other, to settle their disputes or, at least, to overcome various crisis situations. There is a fairly wide spectrum of assistance which the neutrals can provide, as has been demonstrated in practice so far. Suffice it to mention just a few most characteristic types of activities in this respect, such as representation of diplomatic and consular interests (Switzerland fulfills presently sixteen mandates of this kind); peace-keeping operations carried out by the United Nations (European neutrals have taken part in almost all such operations, their representatives and forces playing usually central roles in them); special missions, like the one accomplished by Ambassador Jarring from Sweden in the Middle East in 1967; acting as hosts for various international conferences or negotiations (CD, CSCE, SALT II, INF talks and START in Geneva; MBFR and SALT I in Vienna; SALT I and

CSCE in Helsinki; CDE, i. e. the Conference on Confidence- and Security-Building Measures and Disarmament in Stockholm—to mention just a few well-known examples) and providing sites for headquarters of interntional organizations (Geneva and Vienna, in particular); and, finally, acting as mediators and compromise brokers, especially at some international gatherings in which the East-West dimension is particularly pronounced (e. g. CSCE).

It goes without saying that all this service potential of the European neutrals should not be overestimated. The contributions of these States are obviously of limited effect, short of any essential impact on given situations, especially in the case of deep East-West crises. Nevertheless, they have their particular place in the functioning of the existing system of international relations and do make negotiation and settlement processes develop more easily and in a more efficient way. Modest as this function of the European neutrals may be, it has become a necessary element for the functioning of this system.

Third, in addition to this very useful function of "unobtrusive disponibility", the European neutrals do contribute to peace and security by their own political initiatives and efforts related to some key issues of contemporary international relations.

First of all, the European neutrals, in accordance with their genuine national interests, take an active part in efforts aimed at promoting the process of *détente* in Europe, as well as in the world as a whole, both at the bilateral and multilateral level, in particular within CSCE and the United Nations (unlike Sweden, Austria and Finland, Switzerland is not a member of the United Nations, but has the status of an observer). Their initiatives of this kind—which usually take place in a parallel and complementary way with those of the non-aligned States, and which within the CSCE framework converge in a joint effort with those of the European non-aligned States—have a certain political weight and practical value which are to be acknowledged. The most notable example of this kind is CSCE, in which these States have played an important role from the very outset up to now.

Next to be mentioned in this context is the pacific settlement of disputes which, by the very nature of these States and their international position, is the subject to which they attach great importance. In addition to the already mentioned practical steps they take on various occasions in this field, European neutrals also take important initiatives designed to improve and make more effective the existing system of peaceful settlement of disputes under international law. The best example is the Swiss initiative to this end within CSCE.

Furthermore, disarmament is a field of outstanding importance in which European neutrals are very much engaged (mainly in cooperation with non-aligned States). In the United Nations and in the Geneva Committee on Disarmament as well as within CSCE and its follow-up process, their intiatives are numerous and play a role which has to be appreciated. Sweden is a neutral State which has a particularly impressive record in this matter.

Finally, the problem of the North-South relationship and the question of establishing a New International Economic Order constitute still another important field in which European neutrals play an active and very positive role. Their approaches to this problem are among the most constructive and progressive within the industrially developed world. This includes—especially in the case of Sweden, then Finland and others—the so-called disarmament for development approach, of which they are strong advocates. It is worthwhile pointing out that this policy line in the field of disarmament and development is widely supported by public opinion in these countries.

These activities of the European neutrals in international relations, that is to say their active engagement in international efforts for attaining the above-mentioned political aims, give a new dimension, a new quality to their status of permanent neutrality. Thus they contribute to the cause of peace and security not only by performing their function of "unobtrusive disponibility", which is certainly useful, but also by exerting positive political efforts to this end.

There is one rather special aspect of the European neutrals' activities which deserves particular attention. This is their collective effort within the CSCE framework, carried out jointly with European non-aligned States—Cyprus, Malta and Yugoslavia (the so-called n + n group). One might perhaps go even so far as to say that CSCE constitutes the framework which enables these States to make their most effective contribution to peace and security, first of all in Europe. If their role in this respect is to be strengthened and further developed, then the basic field to build on would be just the CSCE framework, or more precisely the joint action of the European neutral and non-aligned States within it. The emergence of this action group of countries is a phenomen of far-reaching importance. This is a coordinated, joint effort along the non-bloc line; it represents, in a broader sense, non-alignment in action in Europe. The Conference on Confidence- and Security-Building Measures (within the framework of the CSCE) which began in Stockholm in January 1984 is a new opportunity and a new test of these States' ability to make their most effective contribution to the promotion of peace and security.

This joint effort within the CSCE framework combines in itself both mediation and good offices, on the one hand, and autonomous political initiatives or actions of the "n + n" countries, on the other. Accordingly, the European neutrals now appear not only as a factor which helps to bridge gaps and strike compromises, but at the same time they are pursuing political objectives of their own and taking corresponding initiatives. With CSCE the European neutrals have entered a new phase in their peace- and security-promoting activity, and this has involved them in a broader, world-wide effort along the line of non-alignment. It is no longer just peace (-keeping, -restoring etc.) actions on an *ad hoc* basis in which they take part but a long-term endeavor aimed at far-reaching changes in international relations. The European neutrals, through their actions within the CSCE process, together with European non-aligned countries, have become an active factor at the European level and thereby on a wider scale as well. It is an effort, in the long run, for overcoming bloc divisions and thus for promoting peace and security on an over-all cooperative basis and on a footing of equality.

Yugoslavia highly values the cooperation and collective efforts of the European neutral and non-aligned countries within the CSCE framework. This is fully reflected in the statement made by its Federal Secretary for Foreign Affairs Mr. Lazar Mojsov in the closing phase of the CSCE Madrid Meeting (8 September 1983) where he said:

"The neutral and non-aligned countries have asserted themselves once again here in Madrid as an important political factor of the CSCE process. The cooperation of these countries throughout the Meeting and the undeniable results achieved in Madrid, owing also to their efforts, reaffirmed their constructive role. The dynamic activities and contribution of the neutral and non-aligned countries strengthened the all-European dimension and character of CSCE. Their role is important not only for narrowing the differences between East and West, but also for the preservation and promotion of the CSCE process on the authentic foundations of Helsinki. We particularly appreciate the spirit in which the cooperation between these countries was realized, and its results at the Madrid Meeting, especially with respect to the preparation and elaboration of the draft Concluding Document."

This brings us to another point which is also of relevance to further development of the role of the European neutrals—that is, the relationship of these States with non-aligned countries and their Movement. Apart from their bilateral relations with these countries, the European neutrals have established a broader—both formal and *de facto*—cooperative link with this Movement and its members. It is, on the one hand, the participation of the European neutral States as guests at gatherings of the Non-Aligned Movement (first of all the Summit Conferences) and, on the other, their support and contribution to international efforts devoted to resolving the problem of economic development, as well as cooperation with non-aligned States in other matters, such as disarmament, and moral and political support to initiatives searching for solutions to some burning issues, like the Middle East conflict and the crisis in Central America. Naturally, this whole relationship varies in degree from one to another European neutral State and from subject to subject, but it is, on the whole, characteristic of all of them.

All these examples show that in this post-war period the role of the European neutrals in promoting peace and security has undergone a notable evolution and that it has gained in significance. Nevertheless, this role remains of course relatively modest, which is due to the limited power potential of those States, and one should not get the impression that this fact has been overlooked here. The point is that these four, relatively small States perform an undoubtedly useful role in international relations, which exceeds their power potential; moreover, it has been in the ascendancy in the post-World War II period, in particular during the process of *détente.* However, one can also point to certain features in the conduct of their foreign policy which, as seen from our angle, have some limiting effects on their role in international relations or, more precisely, in peace and security promoting efforts.

First, the European neutrals have not always been successful enough in striking the proper balance between their belonging (culturally and ideologically) to the Western world and their status of permanent neutrality—neutrality which also implies their active and special role in international relations along the non-bloc line of action. On the other hand, there have also been situations in which some of the European neutrals, preoccupied with their geopolitical position, have manifested comparatively too much caution, which has had some narrowing effects upon their role in promoting peace and security. Both of the two attitudes detract somewhat from this role of the European neutrals, but it is a matter of judgment, of course, whether it is possible or opportune to act differently in given circumstances.

Next, there is still a certain inclination, expecially on the part of some of the European neutrals, towards a more "neutralistic" approach to controversial situations occurring along the East-West line, such as those manifested within the CSCE framework. If the role of the European neutral States in search of peace and security is to grow, then their initiatives ought to go beyond the traditional level of permanent neutrality. This has been clearly borne out by the experience gained so far, including positive examples of this kind in the CSCE process (e. g. joint initiatives of neutral and non-aligned countries concerning the military aspects of security and the follow-up system, undertaken at the second, Geneva stage of CSCE).

In brief, if the role of the European neutrals in search of peace and security is to be further developed, then they should make further efforts along the path travelled so far in the post-war period. They ought to combine both the traditional component of good offices and mediation, on the one hand, and the new element of taking political initiatives along the non-bloc line of action, on the other. The latter activity, in particular, constitutes an effort parallel and complementary to that of the Non-Aligned Movement, thus leading to closer cooperative contacts and links between the two groups of countries. In Europe, the main field of action will probably remain the CSCE framework, first of all as a joint effort of the European neutral and non-aligned States. This valuable effort deserves special attention and should be further promoted, for which a particular opportunity is afforded by the Stockholm Conference on Confidence- and Security-Building Measures and Disarmament.

Hans Thalberg

Austrian Institute for International Affairs, Laxenburg

The European Neutrals and Regional Stability

1. The Balance of Power in Europe

For nearly 40 years Europe has enjoyed an almost unprecedented period of peace and stability. This is, of course, more true in the West than it is in Eastern Europe, where periodic attempts to escape the influence of the dominant power have brought upheaval and serious setbacks in economic development. Yet even in Eastern Europe the post-war arrangements have, in one way or another, survived with a measure of stability and peace. With all the grumbling about the pre-eminence of the Superpowers, how would post-war Europe have fared if the two Superpowers had withdrawn after the end of hostilities and left our continent to itself? It is at least an interesting subject for speculation.

The profound changes on the European map, wrought by the Allies at the end of World War II, have been formally reconfirmed in Helsinki in 1975; no one, West or East of the new demarcation line drawn at Yalta, is today prepared to challenge the European situation in earnest. There are no issues worth fighting a war for. Of course, there may be an unexpected explosion within the confines of the huge Soviet empire including the Eastern European allies; there may also arise a conflict in the Middle East, or anywhere else in the Mediterranean basin, seriously affecting the European situation. But at this point a European war in the context of an East-West conflict seems remote.

2. The Current Meaning of Neutrality in Europe

As a consequence of this situation, the conceptions and the functions of the European neutrals are undergoing basic changes. Neutrality originally meant non-involvement and impartiality in armed conflict. Permanent neutrality, a status enjoyed by Austria and Switzerland, requires freedom from alliances and absence of foreign military bases. Permanent neutrality has also wide implications for the behavior and for the policies of the permanent neutral in times of peace. A country's decision to become neutral, although an expression of its free and sovereign will, is the consequence of political, as well as strategic considerations of vital importance; above all, such a decision is, as a rule, taken in recognition of certain geopolitical and strategic necessities and constraints. The neutral is taking his country and its military potential out of the strategic equation. The permanently neutral country, having pledged its neutrality to the community of nations, is a factor whose actions and reactions on the international scene can be foreseen and calculated; and therefore it becomes an element of stability in world affairs.

The present situation in Europe offers the neutrals comfort as well as a disturbing outlook for their own future. On the one hand, there is no armed European conflict in sight. On the other hand, should a major war break out, the neutrals know that modern warfare will hardly spare their population or their cities from the spin-off of that war; nuclear weapons with their fallout do not respect neutral borders.

Given the present situation in Europe, the policies of the neutral States are concentrating on lessening international tension, strengthening local and regional stability and eliminating points of international friction; the weight of neutrality has shifted from the legal-military to the political component. Austria and Sweden were the first of the European neutrals to speak of and practice active neutrality, meaning a policy in which all the assets at the command of a small, democratic, industrialized neutral State are to be mobilized for the preservation of peaceful relations and, above all, for the strengthening of regional stability. For regional stability is the point of departure for any peaceful development local, as well as global. The activity of the European neutrals within the framework of CSCE is a good example of this new role of neutrality.

3. The European Neutrals

Austria's permanent neutrality, designed after the Swiss model, has proved highly successful internationally as well as internally, as a focus of national identity and self-esteem for the population of a small country in a most difficult and exposed situation. The Central European Danubian basin, for centuries a breeding ground of discord and war—both World Wars started in and around Austria—has become one of the most peaceful regions in Europe. The peaceful exchange of persons and goods across the East-West demarcation line has become a reality between Austria, Hungary and Yugoslavia, long bitter adversaries in European politics. Even in the difficult years of 1956 (Hungarian uprising) and 1968 (Warsaw Pact invasion of Czechoslovakia) Austrian neutrality has given proof of its solid foundations; no other neutral country in Europe has been put to such harsh and severe tests after World War II. Of course, good luck as well as political subtlety were required in order to weather the storms that swept the area in those trying years. Yet Austria's neutrality has shown its practicability and its intrinsic worth as an element of peaceful development in Central Europe. Austria's traditional roots in Central and Danubian Europe naturally are of help in her relatively new position as a neutral of Western democratic orientation in the Danubian basin. Both Moscow and Washington presently seem to consider the Danubian region as unproblematic and essentially peaceful.

Finland's neutrality serves a most important purpose in the context of Scandinavian security. It tempers the giant shadow which the Soviet colossus throws over the Northern tier of Western Europe. The Treaty of Friendship, Cooperation and Mutual Assistance between Finland and the Soviet Union may considerably complicate things for the Finnish Government; but it in no way impairs the vital service that Helsinki is rendering European security in general. Finland's neutrality has turned a geographic point of potential conflict in a region of strategic importance into a peaceful area. It has given Finland the possibility to play an important and constructive role in the spectrum of European politics. The Western Alliance has every reason to be grateful for the Finnish position. The use of the term "Finlandization", meant to downgrade Finnish neutrality, reveals a basic lack of understanding: it is only natural that a small, vulnerable country should try to adapt itself to its geopolitical situation, to the circumstances of its existence as a nation-State in an unfriendly or even hostile environment.

The neutrality of Sweden, better to say Sweden's pragmatic policy of "not-alliance", is bolstering Finnish neutrality, and is thereby vital for the security of all Nordic countries. Together, Sweden and Finland so far have made it possible, by way of their neutral positions, to keep Norway and Denmark denuclearized; this alone is of high importance not only for Oslo and Copenhagen but also for European security at large. The whole complex of Nordic cooperation, which Europe has come to accept as a cornerstone of European security, hinges on the neutral policies followed by both Finland and Sweden.

Switzerland's permanent neutrality is remarkable not only for its historic roots, going back over four centuries, but also for its unique international setting. Situated exclusively among like-minded countries of Western orientation, she is far removed from East-West rivalries and has little to fear for herself. Switzerland is the only "neutral neutral" in Europe insofar as she is distant from any potential conflict area. She practices neutrality for neutrality's sake. In the Declaration signed by the Great Powers in Paris on 20 November 1815 Swiss neutrality was characterized as being in the interest of all of Europe. Switzerland is concentrating on the services that her neutrality can render Europe and world peace in general by offering mediation and good offices and serving as seat for international organizations and conferences.

4. The Political Dimensions of Neutrality

One aspect of neutrality, politically today the most important one, consists in creating zones of regional stability in a Cold War atmosphere. It is a truism that *détente* is indivisible in the sense that there cannot be relaxation in Europe while Superpower conflict is going on in the Third World; this may be so in a global sense, but happily there are regional exceptions. As has been said before, Finland and Sweden have created an area of stability in Scandinavia and—even more surprisingly—Austria, Hungary and Yugoslavia were able to build bridges of *détente* across the East-West dividing line. Switzerland together with Austria forms a belt of permanently neutral countries that reaches from the French border to the frontiers of Hungary.

These zones of regional stability are based upon mutual neighboring interests, upon the conviction that there are common concerns among smaller European States. It should be noted here that East European countries appear to be at least as much attracted to the idea of regional *détente* as are small members of the Western Alliance. The existence of such zones of relaxation in the midst of Cold War activities and of rhetorics of mutual destruction, areas in which Eastern as well as Western participants find it possible to maintain their respective social systems without becoming deadly hostile antagonists, is a hopeful sign and would deserve more attention and closer scrutiny from the world community and particularly from the Superpowers than it now receives.

5. The Functional Services of the European Neutrals

There exists a wide spectrum of practical services that European neutrals are prepared to offer to antagonists in areas of conflict as well as to the community of nations at large. Good offices, mediation and arbitration are valuable instruments of neutral activity. The exchange of prisoners, caring for the sick, the right of asylum and the resulting provisions for refugees have become indispensable services provided by the European neutrals. The preservation of human rights and of human dignity, briefly the protection of humanitarian interests as well as peace-keeping operations in a divided world, are the cornerstone of neutral policies. Meeting places for international conferences, for peace-making as well as for discreet diplomatic activities, are offered by the European neutrals. Neutral States have become headquarters of international organizations.

To be available for all efforts conducive to peace and stability is an important part of the role played by the European neutrals. Switzerland in particular has a long tradition of serving the cause of peace directly or indirectly by offering Swiss territory and Swiss institutions for that purpose. The International Red Cross, an institution founded by the Swiss humanist Henry Dunant, who had been witness to the carnage of the battle of Solferino in 1859, has become the indispensable center of a wide spectrum of humanitarian activities.

Of course, such services of the European neutrals have become important for the neutrals themselves. To be the site of international organizations and conferences bestows a number of advantages, such as added political importance and therewith additional security, upon the host countries. Austria, in particular, has made efforts in that direction—and Vienna has become the third seat of UN organizations after New York and Geneva. Her traumatic experience in 1938, when German troops were invading the country and the world powers were watching the tragedy without effective reaction, only raising weak protests against the gross violation of international law, against the rape of a peaceful sovereign member of the European community and of the League of Nations—that experience has taught the Austrians that their country needs to move out of the shadow of diplomatic inertia to become a center of international activity.

6. Neutrality as Viewed by Non-Neutrals

As mentioned in the preface of this publication, it was the objective of the Conference held on 27/28 October 1983 in Laxenburg to obtain indications of the assessment and evaluation of neutral functions by other countries, bloc powers as well as non-aligned countries.

On the basis of the papers submitted to that Conference and published in this book, and in the light of the ensuing discussions, it can be said that the appreciation of the stabilizing functions of European neutrals, the creation of regional stability, diminishes with growing geographical distance from the location of such zones of regional stability and local *détente.* As was to be expected, the main interest in the achievements of European neutrals was registered in the countries directly affected by that regional stability. The further removed a country is from the areas of regional stability, the less its interest in and the less its understanding of and affinity to the stabilizing functions of the European neutrals. Neutrals were seen by some participants at the Laxenburg Conference as "free riders" on the train of collective security, trying to profit from the armed shield of NATO without contributing militarily or otherwise to the common defense efforts. Tolerance of the mutually different social systems was regarded by these critics as weakening the position of the Western camp, and cooperation with Eastern Europe was considered a dangerous undertaking. In that regard, the positions of the intransigents in both West and East appear to be almost identical.

7. Washington and Moscow: A Notorious Lack of Policies Concerning the European Neutrals

Whilst Moscow seems to assign the European neutrals a certain place in the policies towards the West, there is notable absence in Washington of any policy in respect of the European neutrals. The lack of interest of successive post-war US administrations in questions of neutrality is notorious. Ever since the founding of the European Communities, Washington hoped that they would become the nucleus for the United States of Europe to which all Western European nations, including the neutrals, were eventually to be attracted.

Notwithstanding the growing problems between the United States and the European Communities in the fields of trade and finances, and the divergent views of the NATO partners in matters of defense policy, Western Europe continues to represent for Washington an almost monolithic bloc of nations: Europe is Brussels, is NATO and EC. There is little room for neutral subtleties, for a different economic grouping of States such as EFTA—even though EFTA policies are noticeably more liberal and therefore more advantageous to US trade interests in Europe than those of the European Communities.

The author of the Soviet paper in this volume calls for a "Europeanization" of European politics; to him European neutrals appear to have the advantage of not being military allies of the United States.

8. A Wider Perspective of Neutral Policies

Neutrality, as presently practiced in Europe, represents a combination of two policies: above all, it is a strategy to defend the neutrals' independence and sovereignty—including the freedom of choice of the social system to which the neutral wishes to belong. Second, it takes account of the principle that no State, notwithstanding its sovereign rights, can hope to exist in freedom and peace without doing justice to its geopolitical surroundings: Finland and Austria, both countries dedicated to the values of Western pluralistic society, have come to recognize the strategic necessity to live in peace with the Eastern Superpower whose armed forces are stationed close to their borders. They will not hesitate to challenge any trespassing of their sovereign rights. They will try to exact a high entrance price from any aggressor. Nor are they willing to submit to political or military pressure. Yet, as Chancellor Julius Raab, a convinced conservative, said in the early 50s, we shall not "twist the bear's tail".

So far, neutrality has been a policy practiced exclusively by countries belonging to the Western social system. There are no rational reasons why that policy could not also be at least tried by countries of communist orientation in certain circumstances. Of course, it would be unrealistic to imagine for a member of an alliance, be it the Warsaw Pact or NATO, to break away and declare itself neutral, because this might indeed upset the delicate balance of forces. But the policy of decoupling ideology from military alliance by becoming neutral might serve in certain sensitive cases, particularly in countries of the Third World, to save or to redress the balance of power in the region. It may be that the United States, inspite of their anticommunist feelings, would be considerably less concerned about Cuba's social system, provided that Havana would take the country openly and reliably out of the Superpowers' military contest. If Cuba refuses to do so and insists on remaining an unsinkable Soviet aircraft carrier pointing its guns against the United States, Nicaragua may be ready in turn to become neutral, to prohibit foreign military bases on its territory and to liquidate military contacts with Cuba and the Soviet Union, whilst adhering to the social system of its own choosing.

It would, indeed, be fascinating to watch whether a State of communist orientation could become militarily neutral or whether the Soviet (and/or Cuban) military presence was an integral part of that system.

9. Conclusion

Summing up, it can be argued that the European neutrals, by taking their countries out of potential conflicts, are bringing regional improvements to the international scene. Their possibilities for finding solutions to these conflicts are very limited; however, the creation of regional stability can in itself be a healthy process, possibly radiating beneficial effects far beyond the borders of the neutral States.

Neutrality is by no means a panacea for all situations of international conflict, nor is it applicable to all States regardless of size, historical background and culture. But under very specific circumstances, such as have been created by post-war developments, neutrality can become an element of stability and of peace in certain sub-systems of a conflict-ridden area.

Participants of the Conference

Aćimović L.	Institute of International Politics and Economics, Belgrade
Alting von Geusau F. A. M.	J. F. Kennedy Institute, Center for International Studies, Tilburg
Andrén N.	Swedish Institute of International Affairs, Stockholm
Backlund S.	Former Swedish Ambassador to the Federal Republic of Germany
Bauer R.	The Brookings Institution, Washington D. C.
Benedek W.	University of Graz
Bindschedler R.	University of Bern
Binter J.	Austrian Institute for Peace Research, Stadtschlaining
Birnbaum K. E.	Swedish Institute of International Affairs, Stockholm
Brundtland A. O.	Norwegian Institute of International Affairs, Oslo
Buchsbaum T.	Ministry for Foreign Affairs, Vienna
Bunzl J.	Austrian Institute for International Affairs, Laxenburg
Bütler H.	„Neue Zürcher Zeitung", Zurich
Callaghan B.	Embassy of Ireland, Vienna
Clement C. J.	Embassy of the United States of America, Vienna
Csarmann M.	Austrian Institute for International Affairs, Laxenburg
Danzmayr H.	Ministry of Defense, Vienna
De Segur E.	Ambassador of Costa Rica, Geneva
Djomin V. W.	Embassy of the Union of Soviet Socialist Republics, Vienna
Du Bois P. F.	Institut Universitaire d'Études Européennes, Geneva
Edwards J.	International Institute for Applied Systems Analysis, Laxenburg
Ehrlich W.	Ministry for Foreign Affairs, Vienna
Gärtner H.	Austrian Institute for International Affairs, Laxenburg
Glatzl C.	Vienna
Gömöri E.	„Magyarország", Budapest
Gudenus J.	Ministry of Defense, Vienna
Hafner G.	University of Vienna
Hakovirta H.	University of Tampere
Haymerle H.	Former Secretary-General, Ministry for Foreign Affairs, Vienna

Hinteregger G.	Ministry for Foreign Affairs, Vienna
Hoffmann S.	Harvard University, Cambridge, Mass.
Höll O.	Austrian Institute for International Affairs, Laxenburg
Iloniemi J.	Union Bank of Finland, Helsinki
Isak H.	University of Graz
Köck H.	University of Linz
Kramer H.	University of Vienna; Austrian Institute for International Affairs, Laxenburg
Kronsteiner M.	Vienna
Levcik F.	The Vienna Institute for Comparative Economic Studies, Vienna
Luif P.	Austrian Institute for International Affairs, Laxenburg
Mailath A.	Vienna
Mates L.	Institute of International Politics and Economics, Belgrade
Mlynar Z.	Austrian Institute for International Affairs, Laxenburg
Neuhold Hp.	University of Vienna; Austrian Institute for International Affairs, Laxenburg
Nick S.	Embassy of the Socialist Federal Republic of Yugoslavia, Vienna
Nowotny T.	Ministry for Foreign Affairs, Vienna
Peterlik K.	Ministry for Foreign Affairs, Vienna
Pfusterschmid H.	Diplomatic Academy, Vienna
Polianow N.	International Institute for Peace, Vienna
Posch U.	Ministry for Foreign Affairs, Vienna
Pucher J.	Ministry of Defense, Vienna
Schober K. H.	Former Austrian Ambassador to Washington
Skuhra A.	University of Salzburg
Thalberg H.	Austrian Institute for International Affairs, Laxenburg
Toth W.	Vienna
Unterberger A.	„Die Presse“, Vienna
Valki L.	University of Budapest
Vargas A.	Ministry for Information and Communication, Costa Rica
Verbeek P. J. M.	Embassy of the Kingdom of the Netherlands, Vienna
Verosta S.	University of Vienna
Wagenhofer P.	Austrian Press Agency, Vienna
Wüstenhagen A.	United Nations Information Center, Vienna
Zanetti F.	Ministry for Foreign Affairs, Vienna
Zemanek K.	University of Vienna

PUBLIKATIONEN DES ÖIIP

Das ÖSTERREICHISCHE INSTITUT FÜR INTERNATIONALE POLITIK / AUSTRIAN INSTITUTE FOR INTERNATIONAL AFFAIRS (ÖIIP / AIIA) wurde gegründet, um Probleme der internationalen Politik mit wissenschaftlichen Methoden zu analysieren. Es legt in drei Schriftenreihen Ergebnisse vor, die sich an ein jeweils anderes Publikum wenden. Das noch geringe, jedoch wachsende außenpolitische Bewußtsein der Österreicher soll ebenso gefördert werden, wie es auch einem internationalen Publikum Ergebnisse wissenschaftlicher Politikbetrachtung vorstellen möchte.

Informationen zur Weltpolitik

Kurze, wissenschaftlich fundierte Analysen aktueller Themen der internationalen Politik, die einen breiten Leserkreis ansprechen sollen ....

1 John Bunzl, DIE AUSWIRKUNGEN DER IRANISCHEN REVOLUTION AUF DIE LAGE IM NAHEN OSTEN

2 Heinz Gärtner, DIE EUROKOMMUNISTEN IN WESTEUROPA

3 Paul Luif, DIE BEWEGUNG DER BLOCKFREIEN STAATEN UND ÖSTERREICH

4 Chrstian Krause, DAS KONVENTIONELLE KRÄFTEGLEICHGEWICHT ZWISCHEN OST UND WEST IN EUROPA

5 Heinz Gärtner, HEGEMONIESTRUKTUREN UND KRIEGSURSACHEN

6 Zdenek Mlynar, MÖGLICHKEITEN EINER STABILISIERUNG DES SOZIALPOLITISCHEN SYSTEMS IN POLEN

Forschungsberichte

Ergebnisse abgeschlossener Forschungsarbeiten, die für Spezialisten bestimmt sind ...

1 Shamil Sharaf, DIE ZUKUNFT UND ROLLE DER BESETZTEN PALÄSTINENSISCHEN GEBIETE BEI EINER NAHOSTLÖSUNG

2 Heinz Gärtner - Otmar Höll - Helmut Kramer - Hanspeter Neuhold, INTERNATIONALE BEZIEHUNGEN IN ÖSTERREICH

3 John Bunzl, DIE VEREINIGTEN STAATEN, ISRAEL UND SÜDAFRIKA

4 John Bunzl, ISRAEL UND DIE PALÄSTINENSER

5 Helmut Kramer (Hsg.), ÖSTERREICH IM INTERNATIONALEN SYSTEM

6 Shamil Sharaf, DIE PALÄSTINENSER

The Laxenburg Papers

Ergebnisse abgeschlossener Forschungsarbeiten in englischer Sprache, die sich an ein internationales Publikum wenden ...

1 Karl E. Birnbaum (Hsg.), ARMS CONTROL IN EUROPE: PROBLEMS AND PROSPECTS

2 Otmar Höll, AUSTRIA'S TECHNOLOGICAL DEPENDENCE: BASIC DIMENSIONS AND CURRENT TRENDS

3 Wolf-Dieter Eberwein - Hanspeter Neuhold, THE ADAPTION OF FOREIGN MINISTRIES TO STRUCTURAL CHANGES IN THE INTERNATIONAL SYSTEM

4 Karl E. Birnbaum - Hanspeter Neuhold, NEUTRALITY AND NON-ALIGNMENT IN EUROPE

5 Karl E. Birnbaum (Hsg.), CONFIDENCE BUILDING AND EAST WEST RELATIONS

6 Otmar Höll (Hsg.), SMALL STATES IN EUROPE AND DEPENDENCE

7 Hanspeter Neuhold - Hans Thalberg (Hsg.), THE EUROPEAN NEUTRALS IN INTERNATIONAL AFFAIRS

Die angeführten Bände erhalten Sie bei Ihrem Buchhändler !